BUSINESS SKILLS FOR CREATIVE SOULS

THE Montreal Artist's Handbook

Youth Employment Services
Services d'emploi pour les jeunes

Youth Employment Services (YES) is a non-profit community organization that delivers English-language job-search and employment services to Quebecers. It offers a broad range of employment-related programs, including an Entrepreneurship Program for those looking to start or grow their own business and an Artists' Program, which is designed to help artists find work or create their own employment opportunities.

Youth Employment Services (YES)
630 René-Lévesque Blvd. West, Suite 185
Montreal, QC H3B 1S6

Tel.: (514) 878-9788
Fax: (514) 878-9950

www.yesmontreal.ca
info@yesmontreal.ca

BUSINESS SKILLS FOR CREATIVE SOULS

THE Montreal Artist's Handbook

Youth Employment Services
Services d'emploi pour les jeunes

BUSINESS SKILLS FOR CREATIVE SOULS:
THE MONTREAL ARTIST'S HANDBOOK

Published by YES Montreal
630 René-Lévesque Blvd. W., Suite 185
Montreal, QC H3B 1S6
Telephone: (514) 878-9788
Fax: (514) 878-9950
E-mail: info@yesmontreal.ca

Business Skills for Creative Souls: The Montreal Artist's Handbook seeks to assist artists by providing information which may help them establish their artistic careers and businesses. The opinions contained herein are those of the individuals expressing them only and consequently, neither the contributors nor Youth Employment Services shall be held liable for any error therein or damages resulting from the use or transmission of said information.

Library and Archives Canada Cataloguing in Publication

Business skills for creative souls : the Montreal artist's
handbook / YES Montréal.

ISBN 0-9681946-3-X

1. Art--Marketing--Québec (Province)--Montréal. 2. Art--Vocational
guidance--Québec (Province)--Montréal. I. YES Montréal.
N8353.B88 2004   706'.8   C2004-905002-8

Printed in Canada.
Book design and typesetting by Les sens créatifs, Montreal.

YES Montreal acknowledges the generous support of les Fonds Jeunesse Québec in the production of this book.

TABLE OF CONTENTS

LETTER FROM THE PRESIDENTS

Over the past decade, Youth Employment Services (YES) has earned an enviable reputation for delivering a wide range of high-quality employment and entrepreneurship services to young people from Montreal and across the province. While addressing the needs of those "looking for a job" or "wanting to start a business", these programs did not directly respond to the unique challenges that face young artists.

Five years ago, based on the above realization, we launched our first program targeted to young artists – a conference entitled "Business Skills for Creative Souls". In the years that followed, the "Artist's Series" of workshops, programs and the annual conference have grown exponentially! It is clear that there was, and continues to be, a real need by artists to develop tools, skills and inspiration that can help them build a rewarding livelihood from their particular talent.

This handbook is designed to be a roadmap for young artists starting out and reaching out. It provides a set of practical skills and advice in critical areas. Also, based upon a highly acclaimed series of YES workshops, the handbook distils insight and advice from local artists who have been particularly successful, and in many cases internationally renowned, in their fields.

The handbook has been a collaborative effort of many people within YES as well as artists and subject matter experts who have so generously donated their time and expertise to make this one-of-a-kind book a reality. We personally thank all those involved for their contribution to this valuable resource!

The book is ultimately designed to help artists, in the largest sense of the word, start off on the right path and with the right tools. We sincerely hope that it will help in your personal journey and to reach your dreams.

Sincerely,

Angela Burlton
President, Youth Employment Services

Charles B. Crawford
Past-President, Youth Employment Services

FOREWORD

By Andy Nulman

True story.

Years ago, when it wasn't at all cool to be a fashion designer, my uncle wanted to be one. His mother, my grandmother, was understandably aghast. "A what?" she cried. "Oy, why don't you become something stable, like an accountant or a lawyer?"

"Don't worry Mom," he replied. "When I'm a successful designer, I'll HIRE accountants and lawyers."

Ah, the dreams of an artist—fame, fortune, and manservants. But if you're holding this book, chances are at least two of the aforementioned three have eluded you. For now, at least.

So until that day when you are surrounded by an entourage of sycophants and experts, *Business Skills for Creative Souls* is the next best thing. More than a mere book, consider this tome a chastity belt for your psyche; use it properly and you won't get screwed.

One of the problems I've encountered in my close to (sigh...) 30 years in the arts is that while every banker, dentist or plumber thinks he is a showbiz maven, at the ready with explanations on what's funny and what sucks, rare is the artist who would even venture to comment on the benefits of deferred debentures or the risks of shorting a stock. And that's too bad, because at their roots, commerce and content are closer bedfellows than most of us would want to admit. Who wouldn't agree that deep inside every trial lawyer is a frustrated thespian, longing to play for an audience far larger than their usual Fringe Festival-sized crowd of 12? And who can ever be more creative than the accountants of companies like Enron or Worldcom, who are to numbers what Cirque du Soleil contortionists are to spinal cords. Remember, as Donald Trump said, it's the "art" of the deal, not the "business" of it.

So don't pooh-pooh the stuff inside these pages. Try it. You may like it. The "dark side" may even consume you, as it did a comedian I once toured with, who met raving backstage accolades after a triumphant show at Carnegie Hall with a curt: "Forget that. How many t-shirts did we sell?"

Well, maybe you don't have to go that far, but when it comes to furthering the deal side of your art folks, the choice is simple—either you follow the fundamentals outlined here, or develop an affinity for cigar-chomping overweight balding guys in bad suits. And then learn how to say "ouch." Often.

Andy Nulman is the President of Airborne Entertainment, and the former CEO of the Just For Laughs Comedy Festival

BUSINESS SKILLS FOR CREATIVE SOULS:
THE MONTREAL ARTIST'S HANDBOOK
BOOK ADVISORY COMMITTEE

Robert Gervais
Mitch Joel
Susan Molnar
Iris Unger

PRODUCTION TEAM

Creative Director/Career Counsellor
Susan Molnar

Head Writer
Caralee Salomon

Writer, Legal Section
Nancy Cleman
Sternthal Katznelson Montigny

Project Coordinator/Editor
Mark Shainblum

Editor/Interviewer
Danielle Pitl

Graphic Design and Typesetting
Rachel Stephan/Les sens créatifs, inc.

CONTRIBUTORS

YES Montreal would like to express its gratitude to the many people who have given
generously of their time and expertise to help make this book possible. They agreed to
be interviewed, provided insight and have spoken at YES events that inspired elements
of this book:

Afsana Amasry	Serge Assadourian	Vito Balenzano
Eli Batalion	Marnie Blanshay	Bless
Angela Burlton	Marion Cameron	Sara Cameron
Chuck Childs	Nancy Cleman	Penny Cousineau-Levine
Marc Dadouche	Denis Dulude	Suzanne Duranceau
Sara Eldor	Jamie Elman	Andrew Elvish
Steve Galluccio	Robert Gervais	Line Giasson
Margie Gillis	Margaret Goldik	Ève Gravel
Mary Harris	Jose Holder	Mitch Joel
Ursula Jugel	David Allan King	Lorraine Klaasen
Tom Kouri	Mark Krupa	Derek Lengwenus
Barbara Lewis	Christina Manolescu	Maureen Marovitch

Josée Nadeau
Susan Pepler
Jacquie Rourke
James Salomon
Paul Shore
Rachel Stephan
Jonathan Veilleux

Andy Nulman
Hilary Radley
Linda Rutenberg
Sugar Sammy
James Simon
Tom Stowe
Jane Wheeler

Leila Peltosaari
Tim Rideout
Solana Ryan
Gary Saxe
Ezra Soiferman
Nadya Toto
Stephanie Whittaker

YES STAFF

Fernanda Amaro
Nicole D' Silva
Angie Foster
Shant Kancachian
Cathy Nguli

Linda Bell
Quincy Davidson
Sherry Hollinger
Monica de Liz
Iris Unger

Louise Anne Coté
Ryan Escott
Tara de Jonge
Susan Molnar

Special Thanks To:

Angela Burlton
Alcan
Charlie Crawford
Fonds Jeunesse Québec
Nicolas Morand
Derek Cassoff

We have attempted to acknowledge all those involved, and we regret any accidental omissions.

GETTING STARTED

LESSONS FROM A CAREER COUNSELLOR

It needs to be said from the beginning: being an artist isn't like being an accountant or an auto mechanic or even a CEO. Those are professions. Auto mechanics may love nothing better than the feel of stripping down an engine and accountants may sometimes dream in Excel spreadsheets, but artists are called to a way of life.

However, art is also a job and it's entirely possible to earn a living creating the art you love, as long as you are willing to be both an artist and a business-person.

Art is subjective

A good accountant saves you money at tax time and a bad accountant gets you audited. Unfortunately, artists have no such benchmarks. Subjectivity leads to doubt. "Am I a good artist? Is my art worthwhile? Will the critics love me or hate me?" On top of this aesthetic stress, artists must also contend with the instability and insecurity that come with the self-employed lifestyle. Their career choices are often not validated by parents, peers and guidance counsellors. Moreover, artists are often poorly remunerated by employers and freelance clients. As a result, many artists approach the nuts-and-bolts, selling and invoicing sides of their careers half-heartedly: they give it a shot.

However, it takes a lot more than a shot to make it in the arts; it takes a lifetime of dedication and passion. Becoming a professional artist is not for the fainthearted.

Artists value freedom and self-expression

This may be a blessing or a curse. On the one hand, you need to think unconventionally in order to create something out of the ordinary; being a free thinker is vital to your craft. But what happens if a client wants to limit your freedom and self-expression by imposing deadlines and requesting content changes? What will you do then?

Perhaps one of the most appealing aspects of self-employment is being your own boss and single-handedly making decisions about every aspect of your business: product design, marketing and distribution strategies, which clients to approach, what time to start and finish your day, what your office space will look like. Great! So far so good!

The flip side of not having a boss is that you need to be the boss. You need to impose structure on yourself, create a plan and follow through with it. Self-discipline is at the heart of any successful venture, because if you don't do it, it won't get done. If you do not follow through, chances are you won't be able to make a living from your artistic endeavours.

Being creative isn't enough
Before you give up your day job, you need to figure out if you have what it takes to support yourself financially through your artistic endeavours. If talent was the primary predictor of success, you would not need this book. We've all heard of extremely talented artists who were unable to turn their talent into cash.

Being creative is not enough. You need to write business plans, price, market and sell your work, negotiate contracts, finance your project, keep track of your expenses and learn how to protect your legal rights. Unfortunately, most arts programs generally do a very poor job of preparing writers, illustrators, actors, sculptors, musicians and other creators for the hard-boiled realities of making a living as an artist.

It can't be repeated enough: a career in the arts takes more than talent, it takes business know-how. Generally speaking, artists either have talent or they don't, but if you're not a business natural, those skills can be learned. Are you willing to learn?

Welcome to the real world
This handbook is designed to address the challenges emerging artists face as they enter the work world. It is our hope that as you read the sections about marketing, business basics, accounting and law, you will be in a better position to decide where you want to take your artistic aptitude.

We have also gathered nuggets of wisdom from working, professional artists, earned over many decades of living the challenges you now face. If success is possible for them, it is possible for you. Make them proud; stake your claim to fame and fortune.

EMPLOYMENT BASICS
GUIDELINES TO DEVELOPING A JOB-SEARCH STRATEGY

Why do you want to work anyway?
People in traditional jobs often make a distinction between "work" and "life" that creative types simply don't understand. However, even bus drivers and account executives need more from their jobs than a weekly paycheck. For artists, this is doubly true. All work should inspire you to dream big and take action, but creative work must have commitment and purpose at its core.

Work also provides social contact, structure and an opportunity to experience a sense of accomplishment from a job well done. It is a forum in which to discover talents, to express creativity and be appreciated. Everyone needs to be a part of something larger than themselves, to do something meaningful, to use their lives well.

LOOKING FOR WORK IN THE ARTS?
Your quest to find your Work Tribe
If you've looked for work at any level over the last few years, you've probably discovered that most job openings are never advertised in the "Help Wanted" section of your local newspaper. Most people find employment through the so-called "hidden job market," which basically translates as personal connections and word of mouth referrals. The only way to tap this unofficial treasure trove of employment information is to develop a strategy: how are you going to create a network and meet people already working in your field or in closely related fields?

Networking at its best
The first step of an efficient job-search is to find your "Work Tribe". This group is made up of fellow artists who you admire and respect, and who share your values and interests. Seeking out your Work Tribe is networking in its purest form, and there's nothing phoney or fake about it. Meaningful relationships are based on giving, not receiving. Focus on getting to know people and building relationships. Job referrals will come in time, but searching for your tribe is about more than just that.

How do you find your people?
Get in touch with your alumni association and see what past graduates are up to. Attend events, audit classes, ask everyone you know for potential contacts (teachers, neighbours, distant relatives, bank tellers, depanneur owners, doctors, dentists). Someone will know someone you can speak to and eventually, this type of networking could lead to your next job offer.

Informational interview

Find people whose work you admire and ask them if they would be willing to meet with you for a half hour to discuss their career paths, their take on the industry and the local market. Ask them for their secrets to success, how they got their first break, any tips they have for someone entering the field, which events to go to, books to read, associations to join, people to talk to, etc. In employment speak, this is known as an informational interview.

Here is some general advice you should consider before you approach your first informational interview:

- When you call to set up an appointment or to introduce yourself, always give people options. Ask if it's a convenient time before launching into your spiel. Offer to call back if it's not. Perhaps they'd prefer a phone call or an e-mail to a face-to-face meeting. Remember, you are asking for a favour.

- The chances of reaching someone by phone on the first try aren't great; be prepared to leave a message. What you say and how you say it will affect your chances of getting a return call. Be upbeat and state the purpose of your call clearly and concisely. Leave your phone number at the end of the message and avoid the normal tendency to speed up when reciting it.

- Your own outgoing voicemail message should be short, sweet and professional. Songs, comedy skits or cutesy messages from your two-year-old niece will irritate busy people and instantly destroy your credibility.

- Be prepared. Make a list of questions that will help you understand your field and teach you how to manoeuvre in it and bring these to the interview.

- Generally, informational interviews are 20 to 30 minutes long. Make sure you stick to the timeline and leave when your time is up.

- Be patient and always thank people for their time. Thank you notes may seem trite, but people really appreciate them.

- Impress the people you approach with your skills. Create something you can send or leave with them that showcases your talent. An interesting postcard, business card or promo gift will remind them of you long after you have gone. The dollar store has many items you can transform. Blank matchbook covers can serve as mini-canvases or business cards. Clothes pegs can be jazzed up and used as paper clips. Be creative; that's what you do best!

- Do not confuse an informational interview with a job interview. You may ask them to take a look at your CV for feedback, but do not give them one unless they ask you for it. It will be obvious to them that you are looking for work; if they can or want to help you, they will. For now, focus on getting information, making a good impression and showing gratitude for their attention.

Volunteer your way to a job

Volunteering is an excellent way to meet people in your field and build a reputation as someone who is reliable, fun to be around and competent. You want to become an indispensable volunteer. Eventually, when an opening does arise, they will want to hire you because they will know you and like you.

- Be strategic about where you volunteer. Look for volunteer opportunities that give you access to a network of artistic professionals that can serve as potential employers, mentors or referees.

- To maximize your network, consider volunteering in several places for fewer hours a day, rather than at one organization, full time.

- Consider the role you will play as a volunteer. Make sure your position allows you to practice your craft to some extent. Strive to be a proactive volunteer: help organize an event, write the newsletter or update their database.

- If you cannot find a volunteer opportunity that suits your purpose, become an independent volunteer. Start a research project of your own that will give you a reason to approach people in your field, a project artists in your community will be interested in. Artists are often isolated; you could start a networking group. Artists often don't know where to find alterative sources of funding; consider compiling a list of corporations that sponsor the arts. Artists need cheap supplies; perhaps you could put together a list of resources. Use your creativity to meet people, to get your foot in the door and to make a great impression.

FIRST STEPS FIRST

Broad strokes

Before you are ready to set realistic employment objectives, you need to assess your strengths, your needs and your expectations. Explore your preferences; what you like to do, what motivates you, and what you have to offer a potential employer. If you don't know what kind of position you want or which organization to approach, start by penciling in the broad strokes. Figure out some basics: would you prefer to work during the day or overnight? Behind the scenes or dealing with the public? In the corporate or non-profit sector? Be clear about what you hope to get out of your next employment opportunity before you start applying for jobs.

Be realistic

Everyone has to start somewhere, usually at the very bottom. If you are applying for internships or entry-level positions, don't expect your job description to be the same as a company's CEO. Young people often have unrealistic expectations; avoid voicing these as much as possible. If you accept your role and responsibilities and you do your job well, you will advance.

Get organized

Get yourself an agenda and a binder to organize your leads, applications, and the business cards you collect. Keep tabs on who you spoke to, the date and their response. Keep a copy of ads you respond to and the CVs and Cover Letters you send to potential employers. Prepare questions you would ask should they call back and catch you off guard, and keep these near the phone.

Research

Before you embark on your intensive quest for employment, gather as much information as possible about your chosen field.

- The best way to get information about the local market is to talk to people in your field. Find out what typical entry-level positions are available. Ask about peak hiring periods so you can apply intensively during these times. Know what local salary ranges are so that you can negotiate an offer without under or over pricing yourself.

- Walk into organizations or companies for which you might like to work and pick up promotional literature, ask about volunteer opportunities and snoop around the office to find out who the best person to contact is. Start building a relationship with the receptionist. Ask for a business card and follow up with a phone call or e-mail.

Set a goal and take action

A plan is a goal with a timeline. As you consider where you would like to end up, work backwards and try to figure out what steps you have to take to get there. Plan out how long it will take to accomplish your goals. Sometimes, your carefully laid plans unravel and you have to go with the flow. Many great careers just happen, especially in the arts. However, deciding on a plan of action is a great way to jump-start your job hunt.

The most important thing to remember when you embark on your job search is to take action. You will create more opportunities for yourself by doing something rather than contemplating vague, intangible goals from the comfort of your living room couch.

Create a list of potential employers

Once you have decided what role you want to play in an organization or a company (grant writer, administrative assistant, curator) you need to identify potential employers. You can use directories, the yellow pages, the Internet, advertised positions and word of mouth referrals. Draft a list of potential employers, and update your list as your search progresses.

Research some more

Research each organization or company you're interested in working for. If you're interested in a specific department or project, find the name of the person in charge. Drop off your application in person if possible. You are in a relationship business. Take every opportunity to help them make the connection between your name, your voice, your great personality and your qualifications.

Make contact

Begin the application process with a phone call. Introduce yourself, and briefly describe your training and experience. Ask key questions about volunteer opportunities, job openings, who to send your CV to and when they recruit. Start building a relationship. If you get someone's voicemail, leave a message. Pique some interest before you send any documentation.

Personalize your application

Tailor your application to fit the position or organization you are interested in applying to. Your CV and cover letter should reflect the research you have done. Emphasize the skills needed for the position, list the software they use, and any other relevant information you can think of.

STRATEGIC CV's

A well-written CV is a key component of any job search. Make sure yours includes:

1. Personal Information

Make sure you provide up-to-date contact information. Getting in touch with you has to be easy. If you mention your e-mail address, make sure you check your e-mails regularly. If you are living with people who may be taking messages for you, make sure you have a reliable system for relaying those messages. If you have an online portfolio or website, include that as well.

2. Highlights of Qualifications or Summary

This section summarizes the key points you want employers to consider. Its content should pique their interest and make them hungry for more. It is your job to know what they are looking for; again, it's crucial that you do your research. List your most relevant work or volunteer experience, the training you received, knowledge (languages, computer skills, other) and personal qualities you may have. Include any accomplishments you are particularly proud of that may not be directly relevant to the position but demonstrate your ability to succeed. If you won an award or excelled in a sport, mention it. Let them know what you are capable of.

3. Relevant Experience

List all relevant experience in chronological order, starting with your most recent experience. Include past employment and freelance and volunteer experiences. For each entry, mention your title on the far left, followed by the company's name and the city where it is located. Include the date on the far right. Describe your relevant tasks in detail using point form. Each description should start with a verb. Organize the job descriptions in an order that reflects the priorities of the position you are applying for.

4. Other Experience

In this section, list all your other work experiences in chronological order. The main purpose of this section is to show that there are no gaps in your work history. For each entry, include your title, the company, city and date. Don't describe what you did there. Going on about waiting tables, for example will detract from the idea that you are a graphic designer and dilute the overall impression you want to make on the reader.

5. Community Involvement

Never describe yourself as a volunteer. Instead, give yourself a title that is relevant to your duties as a volunteer. If you helped organize an event, call yourself an "Assistant Event Coordinator." If the volunteer experience is relevant, describe your duties. If not, it is sufficient to mention your title, the name of the organization, the city and the date.

6. Education

List all relevant training you received in chronological order. Usually, your formal degrees appear in this section. You can also include workshops, conferences and classes that are related to the position you are applying for. Start with each degree's title; don't abbreviate. Mention majors and minors if helpful, then the school, city and date. You may want to add a few bullets to highlight a high GPA, awards won or a thesis title if you think the information is pertinent.

7. Additional Training

List any training you may have that is not directly relevant to the position you are applying for the same way you did in the "Education" portion of your CV.

This may include incomplete programs or other forms of study, such as interest courses or first aid certification.

8. Extracurricular Activities

This section is reserved for activities you were a part of in school, such as team sports, band or yearbook committee. For each entry, mention your title, the name of the team or club, school, city and year.

9. Interests

This is an optional section that mentions your other interests. Employers often look here for the different ways you manage stress and for what else you may bring to your work. If you mention an interest in sports, be specific; list the sports you practice. If you like to read, specify which genre or author you like best. Don't mention the obvious; if you are a painter, you don't need to list "painting" as one of your interests.

As you put together your own CV, here are a few other considerations you should keep in mind:

- Make sure you do not make any grammatical or spelling mistakes; have several people proof read your CV for you.
- One-page CV's are acceptable; if your CV exceeds the two-page mark, it is usually too long.
- Information you provide in a CV should go back about 10 years.
- Always use point form.

- Try to not use the default font (Times New Roman). It is old and tired.

- Watch out for font sizes that are too small.

- Because you are applying for a job in a creative field, strive to put together a CV that really stands out. This doesn't necessarily mean using fancy graphics or cheesy clip-art, but certainly put time and effort into your CV to demonstrate your creative talent.

- It's tempting – and easy – to just blitz dozens of potential employers with the same generic CV, but don't do it! Make sure you understand the specific requirements of each job you apply for, and fine-tune your CV for each employment opportunity.

- Never send your CV to a general "info" e-mail address or to the Human Resources department. Find out who runs the department you're interested in and send your CV directly to this person.

SAMPLE CV

Sandy Pintura
999 Park Avenue, Montreal, Qc, H1H 1H1
Tel: (514) 000-0000 Cell: (514) 000-0000
sandypintura@yesmontreal.ca   www.sandypintura.com

JOB OBJECTIVE: GRAPHIC DESIGNER

Highlights of Qualifications
- 3 years of graphic design experience
- Photoshop, Illustrator, Dreamweaver, QuarkXPress, CAD
- DEC in Creative Arts: Design major
- Bilingual, English/ French, oral/ written
- Ability to meet deadlines, work under pressure, multitask
- Available immediately

Relevant Experience

Freelance Graphic Artist   2001-present
Company A, City
Company B, City
Company C, City
- Consult with clients to establish overall look and content of communication materials
- Determine medium best suited to produce desired visual effect and the most appropriate vehicle for communication
- Prepare sketches, layouts and graphic elements of the subjects to be rendered
- Estimate cost of materials and time to complete project
- Coordinate all aspects of print and audio-visual materials
- Coordinate subcontracting

Illustrator   2003-2004
Company Name, City
- Developed and produced representational sketches and final illustrations, by hand or using CAD, for printed materials
- Adapted existing illustrations

Other Experience

Camp Counsellor   1999-2001
Camp Name, City
Office Clerk   1998-1999
Company Name, City

Community Involvement

Graphic Designer, Organization Name, City, Date
- Designed promotional flyer for fundraising event

Elderly companion, Company Name, City, Date

Education

DEC in Creative Arts: Design Arts   2001
Dawson College, Montréal

Interests

Yoga, fashion design, forensic science

References

On a separate sheet of paper, write down three references. Each entry should include the name of your referee, his or her title, the company's name and this person's contact information (telephone, e-mail, fax). Referees can be past professors, employers or volunteer supervisors. You may choose to put "References and portfolio available upon request" at the bottom of your CV. Let your referees know what positions you have applied for so that they may do a better job of selling you.

When you wrap up a contract, it's always a good idea to ask for a letter of reference. This way, in three years when you apply for a similar contract, if your referee has moved away, you will still have a record of your stellar performance.

Cover Letter Tips

Basically, your CV and cover letter should both summarize relevant information. The Cover Letter is different from the CV in that it allows you to personalize your application and demonstrate your writing style.

Always address it to a specific person and avoid using cold, generic phrases such "as please find attached" or "Dear Sir/Madame."

In your first paragraph, mention the position you are applying for, where and when you saw the ad, and, if you are applying cold, which department you are interested in working in.

The next paragraph should include a summary of your qualifications. You can use the highlights on your CV and simply turn them into a paragraph. You may want to elaborate on your personality, demonstrating key traits with examples.

Finally, you want to thank them for their time and request that they call you to set up an interview or promise to follow up within a week and do so!

Apply

Follow-up

Follow-up is critical, especially when applying cold. From an employer's point of view, follow-up shows interest. Most companies hold your CV for 6 months. Let's assume that at the time of your application, there is no job opening and that one becomes available five months later. If you have not followed up since you sent in your CV five months ago, your CV will have crept to the bottom of the pile and there is little chance they will remember you.

A follow-up plan can be co-created with the person you sent your application to. Let them know you have applied and that you wouldn't want to miss out on any opportunity that may come up. Ask them if it is okay if you touch base about every 4-6 weeks. Ask if they prefer an e-mail or a phone call. Let them buy into the idea. When an opening does arise five months down the road, you will have made several calls or contacts and, because of this, you will most likely be considered, assuming you have been pleasant and appropriate.

Prepare for an interview
Bring several copies of your updated CV and look the part by dressing appropriately. Keep the mood positive and talk about your strengths. Prepare an agenda of what it is you want to let them know about you. At the end of the interview, let them know that you are very interested in the position and ask for a business card for an easy follow-up. Ask them what the next step in the recruitment process will be. Wait for them to call you until the date specified.

Send a thank you note
The day following your interview, send a note thanking them for their time and restating your interest in the position. This shows good time management skills and professionalism. It also reminds them of you and sets you apart from other candidates.

Follow up
Call and ask if the position has been filled. If you were not selected, ask them about how you can improve your chances in the future. Be polite and professional. Keep in mind that they may hire you for another position or refer you to someone they know.

LOOKING FOR A PARALLEL PROFESSION?

The instability and contract-based nature of work in the arts leaves many wondering how to balance career security with their creative pursuits. If finding a "joe job" to pay the rent while you pursue your artistic endeavours is unappealing, you may decide to pursue other interests outside the arts that are equally meaningful to you. You can still operate your business on a part-time basis and claim business expenses, which you will deduct from your other income.

There are many professions in the arts that have stability. Explore these options by speaking with people in the arts, by researching on the Internet and by consulting with a career counsellor.

LOOKING FOR WORK OUTSIDE THE ARTS?

Artists often have multiple income streams, not all of them in the arts. As an artist, you may prefer to find work in the cultural sector, but depending on your financial constraints, you may not have the time it takes to land that perfect job with your ideal Work Tribe. Many artists support their career by working at jobs unrelated to their fields. When you are just getting started as a professional artist, sometimes this reality is unavoidable.

If you find yourself accepting work outside your field, never lose sight of your long term goals and your true identity: you are a writer working as an administrative assistant or a painter working as childcare worker. Do your job well, but don't lose sight of your artistic ambitions, either.

If you decide to accept an offer outside your field, remember that any job can be injected with your creativity. Think of ways you can contribute to the organization once you master the task at hand. Make your mark, add value to the position and make it something better than it was before it found you. Propose to revamp their forms if you are graphically inclined, for example. This is one way to honour your creative spirit and find satisfaction and meaning in your work. People will value your initiative, especially when it makes the workplace a more positive, productive environment. Most importantly, you will enjoy the time you spend there and possibly create a position you will genuinely love.

TAKING STOCK:
SELF-ASSESSMENT EXERCISE

It is obvious that you are passionate about your art; why else would you have chosen an artistic career considering the drawbacks everyone keeps reminding you of? This is an excellent start because your career choice is based on doing what you love.

Next, you'll need to figure out if you are willing to turn your passion into a commercial endeavour. Do you want to express yourself to please yourself or your clients? Can you conceive of doing both? Are you willing to spend a sizable portion of your time promoting your work? Are you comfortable with the idea that you will have to collect and organize receipts, count pennies and stick to budgets?

It is a challenge for many artists to get comfortable with the concept of the bottom line. Before you become a self-employed artist, you need to carefully consider your relationship with money. If you see it as the "root of all evil," odds are you won't succeed at making a profit. If you have an inherent difficulty with the notion of becoming a capitalist and you equate it with being a con-artist, your business venture probably won't succeed.

Be honest with yourself as you complete the following self-assessment exercise to see if you are ready to be a full-time self-employed artist. Perhaps working for someone else is better suited to your personality. You can always operate your self-employment activity part-time and still claim your expenses. And if you want no part of the business side of being an artist, there is always creating art for its own sake and pleasing yourself.

Artistic Business Start-Up Quiz

Are you ready for self-employment? Take this quiz to find out! Answer the questions honestly, and then add your totals. To get the most accurate assessment, first rate yourself then have someone who knows you well rate you.

1. You want to control how much money you make, i.e. the harder you work, the more you make.

⊗Yes ◯No

2. You want independence, to be your own boss and answer to no one but yourself and your customers.

⊗Yes ◯No

3. You want to have flexible working hours, i.e. you don't mind working days, nights, and weekends, as long as you are the one who chooses to do so.

⊗Yes ◯No

4. You are good at making decisions.

⊗Yes ◯No

5. You are willing to volunteer for exposure and building contacts.

⊘Yes ◯No

6. You are confident selling yourself and your art.

◯Yes ⊗No

7. Are you the type of person who is always finding or creating opportunities?

◯Yes ⊗No

8. When you have a good idea or notice an opportunity, do you do something about it - that is, do you seize opportunities?

⊗Yes ◯No

9. Do you like change and look forward to it?

⊘Yes ◯No

10. Do you like to constantly improve things?

⊗Yes ◯No

11. Do you have expertise, a skill, a product or service that is worth buying on the competitive market?

⊗Yes ◯No

12. Have you ever worked in a business like the one you want to start? Do you have previous experience in this industry?

⊗Yes ◯No

13. Do you have a base of contacts and potential future clients who might require your services or product? Enough to keep your business afloat in Year 1?

⊘Yes ⊘No

14. Do you have trustworthy contacts in the legal and accounting professions to assist you?

⊘Yes ⊗No

15. Do you enjoy contract-chasing, sales and negotiating? Wheeling and dealing?

◯Yes ⊗No

16. Do you have savings or someone to financially support you through the rough spots - for at least the first 6 months in business?

⊗Yes ◯No

17. Do you have the moral support of your family or significant other?

⊗Yes ◯No

18. Are you in good physical health?

⊕Yes ◯No

19. Do you have good strong emotional health? Are you able to stay enthusiastic even when the going gets tough?

⊘Yes ⊘No

20. Are you willing and/or able to give up many hours of your personal life to ensure the smooth running of your business?

⊗Yes ◯No

21. Do you like to work alone most of the time? Are you self-reliant?

⊗Yes ◯No

22. Are you organized enough to manage your tasks and prioritize your time? (Remember, no one is watching!)

⊘Yes ◯No

23. Are you disciplined? Do you finish what you start?

⊗Yes ◯No

24. Are you willing to adapt your work to suit your clients' wishes/needs?

⊗Yes ◯No

25. Can you live without the certainty of a regular paycheck?

⊗Yes ◯No

Scoring system
Every "Yes" is worth 4 points. Every "No" is worth 0 points. You will be classified in one of the following categories: 0-49, 50-69, 70-84, or 85-100.

Business Start-up Quiz Results

Quiz created by Peter Johnson and Johanne Larouche, revised by Susan Molnar.
© 2004. All rights reserved.

Business Start-up Quiz Results
- 0-49: It doesn't sound like you are cut out to work on your own at this point in your life. You might be better off working for someone else for now. You can always reconsider this when circumstances are more favourable.

- 50-69: You seem to be lacking some of the qualities, attitudes or proper support. Don't get discouraged. With some work, skill development or a partner who complements your skills you can still do it.

- 70-84: You are capable of making a business succeed. You might want to speak to several people (i.e. counsellors or coaches) and review some of the issues raised in the questionnaire - especially where you answered no - before you begin the process of going out on your own.

- 85-100: Go for it! You are most likely to be successful in business. It sounds like you've got the basic attitudes and characteristics required for successful beginnings and long-term survival.

WHAT'S AN ARTIST TO DO?

HOW TO CREATE BUZZ

Although you are undoubtedly very talented, you are not the only artist in Montreal looking to produce a play or design a line of funky jewellery. Unfortunately, talent alone probably won't be sufficient to distinguish you and your art from the masses. As a self-employed artist, one of the key skills that you must master is the art of effectively marketing yourself and your work.

Let's be honest: until you become red hot on the market, you probably won't have a budget for advertising or a big name agent to peddle your wares. That'll all come with time, strategy and good networking.

Until then, you do have unlimited access to the most powerful tool in a businessperson's arsenal: creativity. This section features tips on getting your name out there, your story talked about and your voice heard.

‾ DEVELOP A PRESS KIT

This is an actual folder that includes several pieces of information about yourself and your work.

Use your innate creativity to develop a design that reflects your personality, your artistic sense and the product or service you wish to sell. If you are not graphically inclined, consider consulting a graphic artist. Although you should thoroughly research the most cost-effective mode of production, your press kit may be one of the few things you need to invest in at this stage.

A basic press kit includes:

- ‾ A one-page biography about you (and your partners, if applicable);
- ‾ An artist's statement: a basic introduction to your art. It should answer the following questions: why you make your art, how you make it, what it's made out of, and what your art means to you;
- ‾ A company backgrounder: a briefing for reporters that includes information about how long you have been in business, who your biggest clients have been, where the reader might have seen your work, awards you have received, etc.;
- ‾ Hard copy and high-resolution images on CD (viewable on both Mac and PC platforms) of your work;
- ‾ News clippings that mention you and your artwork;
- ‾ Contact information for media, clients and investors.

Your press kit is always a work in progress. Add to it as you build up your portfolio and stage successful media events. Rejuvenate it with updated material if your artwork or business takes a detour.

GET THE MEDIA'S ATTENTION

How do you get anyone's attention? By making noise!

A common misconception exists that media types are hostile to PR people. In fact, that's rarely the case. By sending in a well-written press release with a ready-to-go story, you'll be making a reporter's life a lot easier. If you have a high-resolution photo or good videotape B-roll (or beta-roll) to go along with that story, you're saving the news organization a lot more time and money.

Keep in mind that if you want to make the six o'clock news or the morning paper, your press release should contain some, if not all, of the following elements:

- **New:** Did you recently open a gallery, or studio? Are you launching a new magazine? Did you recently publish a book of poetry?

- **Relevant:** News editors look for stories that touch their audience or readership; they want a story that will sell. Tailor your release to the viewing or reading population of the news outlet you are targeting.

For instance, readers of the *Financial Post* will be interested in reading about big name foreign buyers that your first collection of women's wear is attracting; *Flare* magazine readers will want to know why it's cool to wear your clothes; and consumers of the *Journal of Canadian Retail* will want to know what you are bringing to the industry.

- **Entertaining:** Okay, so you aren't bringing the story of the century to the media, but that's no reason to shy away from them. Is there something funny, quirky, or compelling about the piece of work you have produced or the way your business is run? Think about what makes your work entertaining and try to play this angle up both in your press release and in the pitches you deliver to reporters or news editors.

- **Important:** As an artist, you likely feel that you exist to deliver a message to the world. Make sure your passion comes through when you let the media know why you do what you do.

- **Happening:** Time your press release with an event, such as a product launch, book signing, or fashion show and send it along with a personalized invitation to your media contacts the day before and again the morning of the event.

Remember, a press release is not an advertisement. A press release is written in the public's interest, while an advertisement is written in the company's commercial interest. Decide why the public would benefit from knowing your story and build your media release around that.

HOW TO WRITE A MEDIA RELEASE : THE 5WS AND 1H

If you want to grab the media's attention with your press release, it needs to be crisp, sharp and to the point.

Editors usually assume a news story takes the form of an inverted triangle: the most important information goes at the top, while the least important information ends up at the bottom of the text. They always cut for length from the bottom up.

Your first paragraph should include as many of the 5Ws and 1H as possible.

- Who?

- What?

- Where?

- When?

- Why?

- How?

Example: "(WHO?) Jane Doe and John Smith (WHAT?) announce the launch of the first-ever 'Graphic Design Expo for AIDS Awareness' (WHY?) in honour of the late Keith Taylor, former partner at Taylor, Doe and Smith Designs. (WHEN?) The Expo takes place on March 10, 2008 (WHERE?) at Parc Lafontaine and will begin at 2 p.m. (HOW?) with a digital retrospective of Taylor's work as an artist and AIDS activist."

THE BODY OF THE RELEASE

Any other information about your story or event should follow the lead paragraph.

This includes:

- A brief quote from the CEO or event organizer (yes, you can quote yourself but refer to yourself in the third person);

- Additional information about the business (what the company does, what industries it serves, who else is on the team) or about the event (what kinds of activities are planned, anyone of note that will be in attendance, photo and video opportunities);

- Contact information, including phone number and e-mail address.

You should use simple words and short phrases, and write in the active voice to keep it interesting and to the point. Remember to keep the most important facts near the top of the release.

NEWS

FOR IMMEDIATE RELEASE

Youth Employment Services media contact: Joe Wright
Communications Director
514.878.9788
xx@yesmontreal.ca

ATTENTION: Researchers, assignment editors, arts editors, business editors, community news editors, events calendars editors.

SUCCESSFUL ARTISTS TEACH THE "ART" OF DOING BUSINESS
'Over 300 participants expected to attend conference'

MONTREAL – June 3, 2004. Successful artists will share the secrets of their success at the 4th Montreal Self-Employed Artists Conference: Business Skills for Creative Souls, to be held on June 7, 2004 from 10 am to 5 pm at the Centaur Theatre.

Hosted by Andy Nulman (Airborne Entertainment), this year's line-up of speakers and presenters reads like a who's who of the Montreal artistic community. Speakers and presenting organizations include Terry Mosher (a.k.a. Aislin), Hilary Radley (fashion designer), Josh Freed (writer), Andrea Kenyon (casting director), Cirque du Soleil, and the Donald K Donald Entertainment Group. The Canada Council for the Arts and the Conseil des arts et des letters du Québec will also be on hand to discuss grant writing tips.

The conference, hosted by Youth Employment Services, is expected to attract more than 300 participants from Montreal's artistic community.

The winner of the 2004 Artist Grant Contest, co-sponsored by YES and La Fondation du maire de Montréal pour la jeunesse, will also be announced at the conference. Joanne Griffith will receive a $5,000 grant to fund her artistic project, an album entitled Yôyê which consists of 12 songs based on love, childhood, and the art of living together. The music is played with Afro-Brazilian accents and the songs are sung in English, French and Portuguese.

About Youth Employment Services
Originally founded in 1993 to assist job seekers, the not-for-profit organization Youth Employment Services quickly noticed a lack of English-language entrepreneurial services for artists in Montreal and the Arts Program was created in 2000. Comprised of a career counsellor, workshops, a resource library and conference, the program assists artists of all ages to find or create meaningful work or self-employment in Quebec.

DEVELOP A MEDIA CONTACT LIST

While you may be most familiar with artsy magazines, journals and 'zines, it is a good idea to develop relationships with other types of media outlets. That way, you can introduce your work to a much wider audience.

There are companies that publish catalogues that list every publication, television and radio station in Canada, but these can be costly to purchase, especially if you are just starting out.

Instead, visit a well-stocked magazine store with a pen and a pad of paper. Go through the racks and pick out the ones in which you'd like to be featured. Take down the name of the publication, the name of the editor and any contact information you can find (e-mail, fax and phone). If you can't find contact coordinates in the magazine itself, you may still be able to find these on the Internet later on.

For newspapers and television, find out the name of the reporter most likely to write about you and your work. Most large newspapers have writers assigned to each of the following beats:

- New business
- Women in business
- Hi-tech
- Fashion
- Art
- Theatre
- Dance
- Film
- Entertainment
- City

If you're planning an event, contact local calendar editors and inquire about having it listed in one of the event calendars that appear throughout the week. It's usually free to have your event listed, but don't be insulted if your event doesn't make it; space is usually limited.

For television and radio stations, in addition to contacting specialized reporters, you should develop a relationship with assignment editors.

Remember: not every story and event tip is appropriate for all news sources, so choose wisely. If a news editor receives too many useless media releases from you, eventually he will stop reading them altogether.

LEARN TO PIGGYBACK

Have you ever noticed how protest groups come out of the woodwork and dominate news coverage whenever a controversial figure visits Montreal? These people have mastered the "piggyback": timing the launch or the telling of a story with the launch or telling of another that has almost guaranteed media coverage.

Here's a great example: A foundation that raises money for elderly residents of Montreal invited a klezmer band to play for residents and staff of a retirement home. The concert was free and was simply meant to raise awareness for the home.

While the concert would have been a success with the residents at any time of the year, its organizers sought to capitalize on the frenzy that envelops the city each summer during the Montreal International Jazz Festival. They planned the concert during the Jazz Fest and sent out media releases inviting reporters to the resident's first annual jazz fest.

The story had all the elements mentioned above: it was local (perfect for local newscast and community papers), different (no other old folk's home had done anything like that), relevant (the jazz fest is the biggest story in the city during its run), important (it was about an issue close to the hearts of many Montrealers: helping the elderly) and it was happening (reporters were invited to broadcast live from the show).

All in all, the concert was a success and the event garnered a huge amount of media coverage for the foundation.

When you organize your own event, think about how you can time it wisely. Keep track of any dignitaries or high profile leaders who might be visiting the city and think about how your message can fit in with the atmosphere the visit generates. As well, keep a list of national holidays and other days of significance. There are a multitude of obscure "Hallmark holidays" that you might be able to use to your advantage.

GO WHERE THE CAMERAS ARE

Let's go back to our previous example of the protesters. For 364 days of the year, nobody hears from them. But leaders of the G8 show up and suddenly, these people are splashed all over every newspaper and TV in town.

Instead of creating their own unique event, they piggyback on a story they know the media will be following closely. They may send an alert to the media advising them of their presence, but they don't usually have to work very hard to get in front of the cameras.

The point is this: don't try to move heaven and earth to bring the media to you. Instead, bring your story to them.

Writer and communications agency co-owner Mitch Joel recalls one of his earliest days at the helm of a now-defunct magazine which he started up with a friend.

After printing up the first edition, the two partners sat in Joel's basement with boxes and boxes of the magazine, idly flipping the channels on the television, wondering how they were going to get all the magazines distributed.

Suddenly, they came upon MusiquePlus, the French-language music station. MusiquePlus was expecting a big name musician at their studios and the cameras were fixed on the throngs of Montrealers lined up outside in the pouring rain, awaiting the star's arrival.

Then, they hit on it. They grabbed some boxes, got in Joel's car and raced down to the TV station. They gave out the magazine to all the poor souls waiting in the rain. The partners returned home and switched on the TV to MusiquePlus. Splashed across the screen were hundreds of copies of the new magazine, as some fans read it while they waited and others used it as protection from the rain.

Without paying an extra cent for advertising, Joel got a few hours of TV coverage on a station targeting his market and picked up some new readers along the way.

As you organize your own event, think of ways that you can take advantage of big media events, like:

- Montreal International Jazz Fest
- Fashion week
- Blue Metropolis
- International conferences, symposia, etc.
- Visits from foreign dignitaries, stars

Also, don't be surprised if the media are no-shows at an event you've planned in Ste. Anne-de-Bellevue on the same day, at the same time as a keynote address given by the president of the World Bank at Hydro-Quebec headquarters downtown. Camera resources and reporters are limited, so don't try to compete. Research upcoming events in advance and work around them if you can't work with them.

MEDIA ADVISORIES AND INVITATIONS

If you are going to plan an event, it's wise to send along a media advisory the day before and the morning of the event, along with your media release. The advisory should be much shorter than your press release and is often most effective when written in point form.

It should include:

- The 5Ws (in point form);
- A list of photo/video opportunities;
- Names of notable individuals who will be attending the event;
- Key people who can be interviewed;
- Suggested interview topics;
- Contact information.

SAMPLE MEDIA INVITATION

MEDIA INVITATION
PHOTO/VIDEO OPPORTUNITIES
Youth Employment Services media contact: Joe Wright
Communications Director
514.878.9788
xx@yesmontreal.ca

ATTENTION: Researchers, assignment editors, arts editors, business editors, community news editors, events calendars editors.

SUCCESSFUL ARTISTS TEACH THE "ART" OF DOING BUSINESS
'Over 300 participants expected to attend conference'

WHAT:
The fourth Montreal Self-Employed Artists Conference: Business Skills for Creative Souls, where successful artists share their secrets to financial success in the creative arts.

WHO:
Several local 'art stars' will be in attendance and available for interviews.

Opportunity to interview:
- Program participants, including local artists from various fields
- Conference director and career counsellor, Susan Molnar
- Director of Youth Employment Services, Iris Unger
- 2004 winner of $5,000 Artist Grant Contest, Joanne Griffith
- Local artists: Terry Mosher, Andrea Kenyon, Hilary Radley, Josh Freed, Andy Nulman
- Representatives from the Canada Council for the Arts and *La Fondation du Maire de Montréal pour la jeunesse*

Photo/Video opportunities include:
- Andy Nulman's opening address
- Presentation of $5,000 grant to 2004 winner of 2004 Artist Grant Contest, Joanne Griffith
- Conference room filled with over 300 Montreal-based aspiring young artists

WHEN:
June 7, 2004 from 10 am to 5 pm

WHERE:
Centaur Theatre
453 St Francois Xavier
Montreal

About Youth Employment Services
Originally founded in 1993 to assist job seekers, the not-for-profit organization Youth Employment Services quickly noticed a lack of English-language entrepreneurial services for artists in Montreal and the Arts Program was created in 2000. Comprised of a career counsellor, workshops, a resource library and conference, the program assists artists of all ages to find or create meaningful work or self-employment in Quebec.

INVITE A PUBLIC FIGURE

One of the best ways to ensure media coverage is to bring in a big name guest. You can almost guarantee a photo in the newspaper or a few seconds of TV coverage if a member of Parliament or the National Assembly, the city mayor or a city councilperson, or the president or chairperson of an important company is in attendance. Think of who might raise the profile of your event. Phone their assistants and find out the best way to send them an invitation.

If you manage to land an important guest, consider asking them to make a few remarks at your event as this is a sure draw for photographers, TV cameras and radio reporters searching for a sound bite. While many people fear their message will get lost if the focus of their event becomes a high-profile politician, consider it as a worthy sacrifice in your ascent towards fame.

CONSIDER VOLUNTEERING OR DONATING YOUR WORK

Even though she has sung for world leaders like Nelson Mandela and played alongside the likes of Ray Charles and Patti LaBelle, Montreal jazz singer Lorraine Klaasen still makes a point of volunteering with local community groups. She says that working at the grassroots level allows her to develop an enormous support network.

Volunteering your time is a great networking opportunity as well as an easy way to build a name and reputation for yourself. Moreover, it is perfectly acceptable to let the media know that you'll be performing at a charity event or that you have recently donated your work for a good cause.

OFFER ALTERNATIVE SOLUTIONS WHEN THE MEDIA CAN'T MAKE IT

Many times, if you have a well-packaged story, the media will cover your event even if they haven't been able to attend.

- Have a photographer on hand to take high-resolution digital photos that you can later e-mail or send on CD to newspapers.

- Have a professionally recorded beta-roll made at your event. This is a videotape sampling (on beta, not VHS) of key moments at the event.

- Call radio program producers and offer an interview. They'll want to know why they should interview you, what is important or interesting about your story and what kinds of things you plan to talk about. Prepare answers for each of these questions before you start contacting them.

- Offer to provide a list of questions for the interviewer and write up good background notes for them.

JOIN AN ORGANIZATION OF LIKE-MINDED, LIKE-EMPLOYED INDIVIDUALS

Research groups that are active in your industry. Find out what their mission is and read up on the issues that concern them.

If you find one with which you can identify, become a member and offer to be a spokesperson for them. As a well-spoken media go-to person, you will bring credibility to yourself, your organization and your art. And you'll get your name in the media an awful lot.

MAKE A PERSONAL WEBSITE

Once you have produced even just a few pieces of which you are really proud, put them online.

Like your press kit, your website should include:

- Personal and company background information;

- Your portfolio: have your work available in JPG format alongside PDF versions, for easy access;

- A list of any important publications in which you've been featured, or any shows or events in which you've participated;

- Have an up-to-date calendar listing places you and you artwork can be seen;

- Contact information, including an e-mail address and a phone number.

P.R. work does not replace advertising, but used wisely, it will definitely contribute to the success of your business. It is particularly attractive for small business owners because it can be done on the cheap and it will give any advertisement campaign an added boost. Think of it this way, if you invest your time and energy wisely in creating buzz around your art, you will get more bang for your buck if you decide to invest in advertisement.

Although the concept of marketing may seem foreign to your artistic soul, it can be a very creative process. As you devise your own marketing strategy, use your creativity to plan an exciting promotional campaign. Infuse everything you do with your talent. And never forget that you are promoting something people will truly benefit from.

ARTS GRANTS: AN IMPORTANT SOURCE OF INCOME

It's sad but true: as an artist, you need money to make money. Whether you're set to make your first feature-length film, or you're intent on publishing a volume of poetry, you'll need money to finance your endeavour and pay the household bills in the meantime.

In this respect, Canadian artists are lucky. Relative to other countries, there is a great deal of money available in the form of grants for both emerging and established artists in Canada. However, it remains that not every project earns a grant. While there is no way of guaranteeing the success of an application, not applying for a grant guarantees that you won't get a penny. The following section provides basic tips and guidelines on applying for funding and answers some frequently asked questions about the process.

Note that the information presented is of a very basic nature and, in most cases, doesn't refer to specific granting agencies. Although the application process is generally similar from one granting agency to another, expect each to have its own requirements.

APPLYING FOR A GRANT

Before you start applying for grants, consider the following guidelines to improve your chances of obtaining the funding you need.

Before you start
- Look for a source of funding that is right for you. Think about what makes you unique, and research grants that relate to you and your art. The more your art conforms to a specific grant's requirements, the better the odds of receiving funding.

- Review eligibility criteria before you begin filling out an application form. Make sure you qualify for every grant you apply for before you invest any of your time.

- Make copies of each application form to use as a practice sheet.

- Make sure you understand the guidelines and that you are clear on the overall application process. Each agency's requirements will be spelled out clearly in a resource guide that accompanies the application package.

- Most agencies have program officers who can answer specific questions; find out in advance who the program officers are and take advantage of their knowledge and expertise.

○ Prepare a summary of essential information you do not want to forget to include in your application package. As you write up your proposal, use it as a checklist.

○ Create a timeline. Remember, the more time you have, the better your application will be.

○ If the application requires letters of support from third parties, ask for them well in advance. Prime your references with information about the granting agency's mission and priorities.

○ There are numerous arts grant application resources available out there; pick up a book on successful grant writing or speak to someone who has successfully applied for a similar grant.

As you write your own proposal, remember...

○ The first paragraph of your proposal is crucial; make sure it shows that your work is original and interesting.

○ Never assume the committee is familiar with your field, your art or your project. Depending on the type of grant you apply for, you might be submitting to a jury of non-artists. Try to use language that is more business-like, less metaphysical. Keep in mind that you need to convince these business-types that they should invest their money in you.

○ Have friends and family review your proposal. Choose people who can bring different perspectives to your project. For example, ask another artist, a businessperson and a person with good writing skills to review your application.

○ Right before you package your application, read through your proposal one last time, paying attention only to details. Did you spell the name of the granting organization correctly? Is everything there? Are all your pages in order?

Follow-up

○ After you send in your proposal, call the agency to make sure they have received your application package.

○ If you don't get the grant you applied for, ask for feedback from the organization. How can you improve your application?

FREQUENTLY ASKED QUESTIONS

Who decides who gets a grant?
Although the selection process varies from one granting agency to another, usually a jury comprised of individuals familiar with the specific milieu of the grant is chosen to evaluate applications.

Where can I find out about organizations that might fund my project?
There is ample information on the Internet about granting agencies and there are also a number of books and other resource materials written on the topic. Research both.

Pay attention to press releases and publicity materials from other artists or arts groups. See who they list as sponsors or who they are presenting "in association with." That will give you a great indication of both specific companies engaged in funding the arts as well as the types of companies that you might consider approaching for funding.

I'd like to approach a corporation or a non-profit organization for funding. How do I know if they have art programs and what kind of art they are likely to fund?
Start by researching the organization's website. If you can't find specific information, there are a few people you can call.

- If you're dealing with an organization that you already know awards grants to artists, call a program officer and discuss your work with them.

- Many large Canadian and multinational corporations have art collections, usually run by professional in-house curators. They are frequently inundated with calls and letters from artists hoping to sell their work to corporate collectors. It may be difficult to get in touch with them, but it's worth it as they are invaluable industry resources.

- If you're unsure about an organization's arts grant and collecting policies, contact the person in charge of their public relations department.

- If a corporation or organization has funded art programs in the past, these will be listed in their annual reports. These reports are public documents and can be obtained simply by requesting them from a receptionist or administrative assistant.

I can't seem to find a granting agency that is right for my project. Where else can I look for funding?

Depending on your planned project, it may be wise to approach organizations that aren't strictly limited to arts funding. For instance, if you are looking to open an interactive art gallery, you could qualify for a business entrepreneurship grant. If you are looking to photograph Canadian national parks and package it as a keepsake calendar, you might qualify for funding from a tourism agency.

I have a large portfolio of my work; some of the samples are very risqué, others are more commercial. Is it better to include more or less in the portfolio?

If your intended project doesn't involve anything risqué or if the agency from which you seek money isn't specifically geared towards non-commercial artists, don't risk putting off the jury with something that might offend them.

Do I need to include a business plan?

Only include a business plan if the granting agency requires one. Before you write your own, we highly recommend that you pick up a book on the topic, or that you consult with a business coach available at some non-profit organizations.

SAMPLE BUSINESS PLAN

ARTIST BUSINESS PLAN

Executive Summary (no more than one page)
Write this section last; this will help you write a well-directed, concise summary.
- Provide a short description of your art work
- Briefly describe your marketing and financial strategy

Artist Statement (about a paragraph)
The artist statement, or your mission statement, is a basic introduction to your art.
- Include basic information about why you create your art, how you create it, and what it means to you.

Description of the Art (1 to 3 pages)
In this section, present a detailed description of your artwork.
- Provide information about yourself, your skills and any previous experience you have had.
- Explain exactly what makes your artwork unique (What types of materials do you use? What does your work look like? Does it serve any kind of practical purpose? How is it made?)
- Include your resume and high-quality images of your art at the end of this section.

Target Buyer (1 page)
This is a detailed description of your target buyer.
- Provide information about your buyers' demographic profile: their gender, their income, their age range, their level of education, their marital status, etc.
- You should also include information about your buyers' psychographic profile: why they buy, how often they buy, when they buy and where they buy.

Marketing your Art (1 to 3 pages)
- Explain what makes you different from other artists in your field, what unique advantages you have in the marketplace.
- Define your advertising and promotion strategies for reaching your target buyer (which tools you will use and how you intend to use them)
- Define your pricing strategy (how much does it cost you to produce your art, what kind of profit margin would you like to make, etc.)
- Define your distribution and sales strategies (will you be selling through a wholesaler? Retail? Private showings?)

Financial Strategy (1 to 3 pages)
- Project your sales and expenses and put them in income statement format
- Include information about sources of financing

Action Plan (1 page)
- Provide a time-line of the various strategies outlined in the plan

Is this a loan? Do I eventually have to pay back the money I received as a grant?
No and no. Grant money is given free and clear and is considered a part of your annual taxable income.

Do I have to pay taxes on the money I've been awarded?
Yes, and be careful! There are no deductions at source; you receive the full amount of the grant and are responsible for paying any taxes you may owe. You will need to declare this money when you file your tax return in April, so make certain to set aside a portion of the grant to pay the taxes on it.

I've received a grant based on a business proposal I submitted, but I've now changed my mind and I have an even better idea. Can I keep the grant money to finance that idea or do I have to follow through with the proposal I submitted to the agency?
Some agencies may be open to allowing this kind of change, but it is best not to start your new project before setting up a meeting with a program officer to discuss the detour.

I have received a grant and things are going really well. I think I'm going to have a surplus of money. Do I have to give the leftover funds back?
No. Again, grant money is yours, free and clear, as long as you fulfill the terms of your application.

Should I acknowledge the grant I've received?
Definitely. Thank-you notes go a long way. Send one to all of the contacts you've developed to show your appreciation and to keep the lines of communication open.

Many granting organizations will also require you to use their name and logo on any promotional material you produce. Also, indicate their support on your professional website and in any press releases you send out about your work.

Why was I denied a grant?
Being told you are ineligible for a grant does not mean your project is not worthwhile. Don't get discouraged. Successful grant applicants usually have been refused several times before they receive a grant.

There are several reasons why applications are turned down. The application process is very stringent; there are exacting guidelines to follow and very precise criteria to be met. You might have erred in a portion of the application, or the jury might have decided that you didn't quite meet the organization's criteria. In the end, quite simply, there may not have been enough money in the pot for everyone.

Where else can I look for sources of funding?
Financial support doesn't only come in the form of cold, hard cash. Consider creating your own funding opportunities. For instance, offer to give free publicity to a print shop in exchange for free posters. Or include a restaurant logo on your launch invitations in exchange for platters of food to be served at the event.

DOS AND DON'TS

- **Do** edit and re-edit your application many times. Time permitting, let your proposal sit for a while, and then work on it again. Taking a step back will give you a new perspective on your proposal.

- Whenever possible, **do** use the application form's exact wording to respond to a question; repeating the question will bring clarity to your proposal.

- **Do** put a lot of thought into your title; it's the very first thing the committee will read and first impressions are crucial.

- **Do** start the writing process early. If you rush it, you risk making mistakes that could cost you the grant.

- **Don't** contort your vision to fit a particularly attractive grant. Be imaginative in your research while trying to find grants for which you are eligible. By staying true to your idea, you'll make a more convincing case for yourself.

- **Don't** inundate the jurors with everything you've ever produced. Present an up-to-date portfolio with your best work.

- **Do** put together a high-quality portfolio; any slides, images, demos, etc. you include should be top-notch.

FIVE MOST IMPORTANT ELEMENTS OF A SUCESSFUL APPLICATION

1. Have a clear idea of your project before you start applying for grants. Make sure you are passionate about it. Conviction goes a long way.

2. Start preparing your application early. If you rush the process, it will definitely show in your work.

3. Although you should strive to conform to the instructions, let your creativity shine through by making your proposal unique and memorable.

4. Clarity in the writing process is paramount. A poorly written or disorganized application will usually not be considered. Make your application legible and easy to understand.

5. Pay attention to detail. You don't want the jury to dismiss your proposal before assessing its content because of minute mistakes such as an incorrectly spelled name.

ARTISTS AND THE LAW

By Nancy Cleman and Xanthoula Konidaris
Sternthal Katznelson Montigny

BASIC POINTS AND PRACTICAL TIPS

The purpose of this chapter is to provide artistic entrepreneurs with some basic legal information and relevant sources, which will be helpful to them in the conduct of their businesses.

The challenge that presents itself for artists, writers, musicians and others is that much of what they try to protect is based on things we cannot see i.e. "intellectual property" (IP), as opposed to tangible property such as tables and chairs. The world of information technology adds countless ways to duplicate material and transmit it in ways which would have been unthinkable in earlier times.

The aim of this chapter is to provide high-level advice of a very general nature. It is focused on artists doing business in Quebec. It does not constitute legal advice. It should be used as a reference only and does not replace the need to contact a lawyer or other professional, as the case may arise.

INTRODUCTION

Artistic entrepreneurs include a large group of people, namely musicians, filmmakers, dancers, writers and painters, among others. While the ways of doing business (e.g,. as a company, partnership or sole proprietorship) are the same as for other types of entrepreneurs, the nature of the business may require special types of protection.

Although this chapter is the legal section, we will try to make it as simple as possible. The goal is to provide you with some basic guidelines and tips on how to carry out your business and protect yourself and your work. One thing you should know about Canadian law is that there are two legal systems: federal and provincial. Quebec is a civil law jurisdiction and has a Civil Code. The rest of Canada is a common law jurisdiction and is based on Common Law. Federal laws apply in all provinces. Federal laws are created by the government of Canada, as opposed to provincial laws which are enacted in each province. Intellectual Property (copyright, trademark, patents, etc.) is governed by federal law for the most part. Doing business, entering into contracts and employment matters are, for the most part, governed by provincial law.

This section will cover three main topics:

    a. Laws of importance to artistic entrepreneurs

    b. Ways of doing business

    c. Contract dos and don'ts

LAWS OF IMPORTANCE TO ARTISTIC ENTREPRENEURS

For most artists a key issue is how to protect their work. In this section we will briefly touch on some of the laws relevant to artists. At the end of the book you will find a bibliography of websites and other references that provide some helpful information. A large part of the discussion will focus on copyright law, because this is of major importance to artists. We also draw your attention to two laws in Quebec that are specifically enacted to protect artists in their dealings with promoters and producers. In addition we will also discuss trademarks. For more information on intellectual property see the Canadian Intellectual Property Office (CIPO) website at www.cipo.gc.ca.

COPYRIGHT (COPYRIGHT ACT CANADA)

What is copyright? As the name implies, copyright represents the right to copy or reproduce a work protected by copyright. This right belongs to the copyright holder to the exclusion of any one else, except for very limited exceptions.

What copyright protects: Copyright protects the expression of an idea but not the idea itself; it includes books, works of art; dramatic works; musical works; sound recordings; performances; broadcast signals; literary works and software programs.

Nature of rights: A copyright holder has exclusive rights for the length of the copyright. These include derivative rights such as translation of the work and making other versions of the work; the copyright holder determines who can use the material and for what purpose(s).

How is copyright obtained? Copyright arises automatically the moment you create an artistic work in a fixed and tangible medium. You can register your copyright with the federal government through the Canadian Intellectual Property Office, but the law does not require it. However, it is useful to have some proof that you came up with the idea since it is possible for two people to own copyrights on similar creations (say, a story idea), provided they can prove they independently came up with the idea. If not, there is a risk that one party will sue the other for infringement, or unauthorized use. It's also not a bad idea to mail a copy of a creative work in which you claim copyright to a trusted advisor with a note to leave it unopened. In the event there is a problem, the sealed and dated letter may help prove when the work was created, and therefore help determine who created the work first.

Copyright gives the holder control over how his work is used. This means the "sole right to produce or reproduce the work or any substantial part thereof in any material form whatever, to perform the work or any substantial part thereof in public, to publish an unpublished work, to translate a work, to convert a dramatic work into a novel or other non dramatic work; to make a novel into a play; to make a record;" etc. (see Section 3.1 of the Copyright Act)

Copyright owners can add a notice to the work to confirm copyright:
© NAME OF OWNER, 2004. ALL RIGHTS RESERVED.

Term: The term of this right is generally the lifetime of the author (the person who created the work) plus 50 years from the end of the calendar year in which the author died (though there are some exceptions to this rule). Copyright arises automatically. Registration provides additional protection in Canada and other countries which belong to the World Trade Organization and international copyright treaties like the Berne Convention, the Universal Copyright Convention and the Rome Convention. Citizens of countries which are members of those conventions enjoy the benefits of Canadian copyright law in Canada.

Sound recordings are also protected in Canada under the Copyright Act, but the protection accorded to sound recordings under international treaties varies considerably from country to country.

Commentary: Copyright protects the expression of an idea but not the idea itself. What is the difference between expression and idea? For example, let's think of a story about a little girl who goes to sleep and wakes up transformed into a cat because her stepbrother put a spell on her. This is the idea. One person can write a story, another may write a screenplay and a third a stage play. These three vehicles are expressions of the idea. If the first thing to be published is the book and from the book someone decides to make a movie or stage a play, the movie and stage play would be derivative works that follow from the book.

Under the Copyright Act a "work" can take many forms. It may be a play, a painting, a literary work, a sculpture or an animated film, but it must be the direct result of the author's labour. It sounds simple, but it can get a little complicated, especially when more than one person is working on an artistic project. Joint authors of a novel would share copyright, but their editor would not, even if his input had an impact on the final product.

Copyright is vital to artists because the copyright holder has the exclusive right to copy, reproduce, translate, dramatize or adapt the work. If you're an author, a publisher must make an arrangement with you before publishing your book. If you're a filmmaker, a film distributor needs to sign a contract with you to have the right to put your film in the theatre. Digital technologies make it extremely easy to copy and distribute your work, so it is important to understand both the legal relation and the technical realities of digital and electronic rights to protect your work and make sure you make money on your work and not let others take advantage of your work.

A key element for copyright to arise is that the expression (be it a song, story, film or other) must be in a fixed and tangible medium of expression. It arises automatically in such a case.

Who owns the copyright? Copyright usually belongs to the author of the work, although there are exceptions. If you create an artistic work on commission, you keep control of the copyright unless you sign a contract explicitly transferring the copyright to the person who commissioned you. It is important to check the rules for your field, i.e., the rules for photographers generally provide that they retain the copyright to their photos even if they are hired by someone else. An artist can sell his painting and still retain the rights to reproduce the work. They cannot stop the buyer from re-selling the work, but they can stop the buyer from reproducing the work on t-shirts or coffee mugs.

However, if you're a full-time employee, your employer owns the copyright to any work created as part of your employment. For example: If you paint an illustration for an advertisement while working for an ad agency, it's the ad agency (or their client) that owns the copyright, not you. Similarly, if you're a staff journalist working for a daily newspaper, any stories you write will belong to the newspaper. Freelance journalists work under a different arrangement, and usually keep their copyrights, because they are independent contractors and not employees.

Employees and consultants: As noted above, your employer owns the copyright of anything you create while working for her. However, if you're a consultant rather than an employee, the copyright stays with you unless your consulting contract states otherwise, so read your contracts carefully before signing!

Make sure you and your employer both understand your legal status before you start to work. Are you an employee or a contractor? Are you keeping your copyrights or assigning them as part of your contract? This is why people are often asked to sign complex employment contracts or letters of agreement that include an assignment of all rights to anything they develop in the course of their employment or engagement. It is very important that you read and ask questions before you sign any agreement so you know what you are giving up and what you are keeping, and at what cost.

Assignment: Assigning copyright means that the author legally turns the ownership of a work over to a third party for a specific fee. Once an assignment has been made, the author no longer owns the work, though he still usually retains his moral rights (see below).

Licensing: Licensing is a less drastic step than assignment. An artist can license a third party to use his work in a specific context for a specific length of time without surrendering ownership of the work. For example, an artist may license a character to an ad agency for use in a TV commercial. The agency may only use the character for that specific purpose, for the length of time specified in the license agreement. Otherwise the artist still controls her image.

INFRINGEMENT

Under the Copyright Act, it is infringement for any person to do anything with a copyrighted property without the consent of the owner. This includes selling, renting and making other works based on the work. This means – for example – that you cannot stage a play based on a best-selling novel without the author's permission. Nor can you make copies of copyrighted CD's or DVD's and sell them to your friends. There are limited "fair dealing" exceptions under the Copyright Act, which allow you to make limited use of someone else's copyrighted work under very specific circumstances. For example, you may use small portions of someone else's work in research, certain types of news coverage and critical reviews. Keep in mind, however, that the rules of fair dealing are complex and what's permissible is limited, so it is a good idea to get permission to use someone's work if you're not sure of your rights.

THE PUBLIC DOMAIN

What is the Public Domain?: Once the copyright on an artistic work has expired, the work falls into the "public domain," that is, it becomes everyone's property. Shakespeare's plays and Beethoven's symphonies are in the public domain in Canada. As noted on the CIPO website, under the Copyright Act, basic facts, ideas and news are also considered part of the public domain. Note of caution: A new work based on the public domain – like a new movie based on *Hamlet*, or a specific performance of a Beethoven symphony – is protected under copyright. Also keep in mind that foreign countries may have different definitions of the public domain, and a work you can legally use in Canada may still be under copyright protection in other jurisdictions.

MORAL RIGHTS

Moral rights are a separate class of intellectual property rights that have been recognized in Canada since 1931. They exist independently of the author's copyright and protect the work's paternity and artistic integrity. Unlike copyright, moral rights cannot be assigned to anyone else, though under certain circumstances the author may agree to sign a waiver agreeing not to insist on his moral rights.

Paternity: The author retains the right to have his name (or pseudonym) associated with a work even if he has sold it or assigned the copyright to someone else.

Integrity: Even if he has assigned the copyright to someone else, moral rights give the author a certain degree of control over any action that "deforms, mutilates or changes" his work in a way that may have a negative effect on his honour or reputation.

Neighbouring Rights: Neighbouring rights are similar to copyright and protect the rights of performers who perform works copyrighted by someone else. Since 1997, the Copyright Act has acknowledged that – for example – a singer has certain intellectual property rights to her performances even if she is singing a song composed by someone else. Performers also receive royalties when their songs are broadcast. Under certain conditions, neighbouring rights also protect record labels and broadcasters.

Neighbouring rights have changed age-old relationships in the recording and music industries. Just as a singer needs to get permission from the composer to perform one of her songs, the composer now must also get permission from the singer to use a recording of her voice. Filmmakers and multimedia producers must also make sure they have all the necessary neighbouring rights clearances when using recorded performances in their productions. Needless to say, this is a new and complex area of the law, and it's advisable to get professional legal advice if you have questions.

PERSONALITY RIGHTS

Personality rights are the rights of individuals to prevent unauthorized commercial use of their name, likeness, or other personal attributes. In Quebec, these are protected by the Civil Code of Quebec and the Quebec Charter of Human Rights. To summarize the articles of the Civil Code, "everyone has a right to have his reputation and privacy respected. No one may invade the privacy of the person unless authorized by law." Using a person's face and/or voice without his consent can constitute an invasion of privacy. The same applies to using the person's likeness, name, voice, or image for a purpose other "than the legitimate information of the public." This also applies to the use of his correspondence, manuscripts, or other personal documents.

Releases: If you are creating a project which uses a person's image, voice or likeness in your work, you should obtain their consent in writing. For example, a filmmaker must get a written permission or release to use a person in his film or video.

Personality rights need to be distinguished from privacy rights. Both federal and provincial legislation address how personal information may be used, but that is beyond the scope of this chapter. For more information, you should contact a legal professional.

SUMMARY TIPS:

1. The author is generally the first owner of the copyright in the work.

2. You may not use someone else's work, image, voice or likeness without their permission.

3. Just because you can technically copy something does not mean that you have the legal right to do so.

4. Assignment gives away your copyright but not your moral rights.

5. Moral rights cannot be assigned, but they can be waived.

6. If you use someone's work without permission, you can be sued for copyright infringement and be subject to pay damages.

7. Read terms of use on websites; put copyright notices on your work and websites.

8. Musical rights can be complex; they include publishing or synchronization rights, recording rights, artist rights, and arrangement rights.

TRADEMARKS (TRADEMARKS ACT CANADA)

What is a trademark?: A trademark can be a word, shape, or symbol used to distinguish the goods and services of one seller from one another. For example, Pepsi®, 7-Up® and Sprite® are trademarks of different types of soft drinks, while Tide®, Cheer® and Sunlight® are laundry detergent trademarks. A trademark is not the same thing as a trade name, which is the name under which a company or an individual carries on business.

How are trademarks protected?: Trademarks can be protected through common law just by use. If you can show that you have used a specific trademark for many years and that the public has come to associate your goods or services with this trademark, you can claim "prior use," if someone else tries to use a similar name or design. However, it is much more advisable to register your trademark with the Canadian Intellectual Property Office, because registered trademarks have much stronger protection under the law.

Trademark registration can be a fairly complex process. It involves filling out an application and awaiting a lengthy review. Acceptance of the application is not guaranteed, especially if someone else objects to your application. It's advisable to seek professional legal help in the trademark registration process.

Term: For registered trademarks, generally the term of the protection is fifteen (15) years and is renewable. If you are using an unregistered trademark, your rights continue as long as you use the mark properly and no one opposes you. If you stop using the mark, however, you risk losing your protection.

Territory: Registering a trademark in Canada does not necessarily give you legal protection in other jurisdictions. You must register your trademark in every country where you plan to do business.

Need to give notice: In Canada, you are required to give notice to the public if you are claiming a trademark. You give notice by putting a TM in superscript near the name. You may sometimes also see the symbol ®, which is another way to note a registered trademark. You can also put an asterisk (*) next to the trademark, which refers to text elsewhere on the package, which explains that it is a trademark you own or license. The trademark owner must also demonstrate some type of control over how the trademark is used and over the quality of goods and services that bear the trademark.

Licensing: If a trademark owner wants to allow a third party to use his trademark, he needs to enter into a written contract such as a license agreement. The license agreement is also the best way for the trademark owner to ensure that his trademark is being used in an appropriate manner.

Use it or lose it: To maintain ownership of a trademark, you must use it and police your rights. You may lose the rights to the trademark if you don't use it. You can also lose your trademark rights if :

    (a) others start using it (or a trademark confusingly similar to yours) without your permission and you do nothing to stop them, or

---

(b) you allow your trademark to become the generic, commonly accepted word for a particular product or service, or

(c) you do not use your trademark properly or allow others to use it improperly or without the appropriate trademark ™ or ® symbols, or

(d) you do not exercise control over the goods or services which the trademark represent.

Common words like cellophane, zipper, and escalator were all trademarks at one time, but their owners lost them to the public domain. An easy rule to remember is in a sentence, use your trademark as an adjective and not a noun. Also provide guidelines to other people you allow to use the trademark, such as colour, font, etc. This is a necessary part of legally protecting your trademark.

Tip: Don't confuse the trademark with the trade name. Establish guidelines for how you want your trademark to be used and make sure it is used accordingly.

Trademarks can be expensive, so do a search before you apply to register the mark. Such a search can be done on the CIPO website, for Canadian trademarks. Make sure you have guidelines for how you want the trademark to be used and its use controlled.

QUEBEC LEGISLATION FOR ARTISTS

The province of Quebec has two pieces of legislation to protect artists. *An Act respecting the professional status and conditions of engagement of performing, recording and film artists* (R.S.Q., c-S.32.1) ("Producers Act") and *An Act respecting the professional status of artists, individual art, arts and craft and literature and their contracts with promoters* (R.S.Q., c-S.32.1). ("Promoters Act")

These Acts cover a number of items. What is important for an artist under the Promoters Act (someone who is a creator in a field of visual arts, arts and craft or literature has a status of a professional artist, if he declares himself to be an artist, produces his own work, and his works are exhibited, produced, published and presented in public and he has been recognized by his peers as a professional artist) are the provisions that govern the artist and promoter. A promoter is a person whose main or secondary activity is to enter into contracts with artists, as a business.

Chapter III of the Act requires that contracts between artist and promoters must be made in two copies and describe the following elements:

1. the nature of the contract;

2. the work or works which form the object of the contract;

3. any transfer of right and any grant of license consented to by artist, the purposes, the term or mode of determination thereof, and the territorial application of such transfer of right and grant of license, and every transfer of title or right of use affecting the work;

4. the transferability or non-transferability to third parties of any license granted to a promoter;

5. the consideration in money due to the artist and when and how it will be paid;

6. the frequency with which the promoter will tell the artist on the transaction made with respect to his work in subject to the contract and for which money remains owing after the contract is signed.

These are the key criteria that an artist should consider whenever he is doing business with someone concerning the sale of his work.

The Act further states the artist is not bound to perform his obligations until such time as he is in possession of copy of the contract. There are also some special clauses with respect to exclusivity. If an artist has a contract with a promoter which reserves for the promoter an exclusive right for future work of the artist or which recognizes the promoter's right to determine the circulation of the work, the contract must identify the work or at least the nature of the work. As well, it must contain clauses that provide a period for the promoter to decide whether or not he or she wants to take the work. The contract has to have clear notice provisions and termination provisions. For example, the artist must have the right to end the contract after notice is given by the artist.

In the case of an artist under the Producers Act, the producer is the person who retains the services of the artist in view of producing or presenting to the public the artistic work in the field of endeavour, which can include opera, theatre, music, dance, variety entertainment, multi-media films, disk, etc.

Under the Act, if a person considers himself an artist who binds himself to one of several producers by way of engagement contracts, he is deemed to practice the art on his own account. An artist is free to join any artist's association and is free to negotiate and agree with the conditions and other engagements by a producer.

An artist and a producer bound by the same group agreement cannot stipulate any condition that is less advantageous for the artist than the group condition.

What this means is that if an artist is a member of a professional association which has certain standard agreements, he cannot negotiate terms and conditions for himself that are less advantageous than the standard agreements negotiated by the group.

WORKING WITH INTELLECTUAL PROPERTY

BASIC TIPS AND TRICKS

Just because an artist is involved in a cultural and creative endeavour does not mean he or she should be creative in doing business. It is beneficial to have some rigour and discipline in entering into agreements, because the consequences can be very important to you at the end of the day.

It is very important, whether or not you hire the services of professional advisors, to understand what you sign. If you don't understand it, ask questions. And remember, there are no stupid questions. If you think you have a problem, you may be right. It is better to take action sooner rather than later. Once you have given your rights away, you may be unable to get them back.

Seek advice from a lawyer or through a professional association.

Another important thing to remember when seeking advice, whether it be from a lawyer, accountant, or professional association, is to tell the person the whole story. This means not what you thought you should have done, could have done, why the other side is wrong, etc. Tell your advisor the facts as you remember them. It is also useful when you think you are getting into a dispute to keep track of events and document facts, names and dates. It is often difficult to remember what happened when things get to Court or arbitration months or years later.

Two common ways of dealing with rights are selling them or licensing them.

ASSIGNMENTS AND OPTIONS

Generally when an artist sells his rights he is asked to sign an assignment, which gives the buyer all rights, title and interest in the work.

Sometimes an artist will give a person an option to purchase certain rights. This is referred to as an option deal. In such a case the purchaser pays a certain amount for the right to purchase the work for a certain period of time. For example an author of a book may give a filmmaker the option to make a movie. The price of the option is one fee and the right to exercise the option, i.e., purchase the rights is another.

LICENSING

As discussed, if you incorporate someone else's work into your own or someone wants to use your work, the two parties should enter into an agreement setting out the terms and conditions of the arrangement. In this section, we will discuss some of the basics of licensing.

There are several issues to be considered in any license agreement:

a. What is the subject matter that is being licensed?

b. Type of license - exclusive vs. non-exclusive

c. Term (months, years)

d. Territory (Canada, US)

e. Scope - i.e. what uses are permitted? (TV, radio, Internet, advertising, etc.)

f. Royalties or license fees (one-time fee, per-use fee, combination of two; percentage of sales)

COLLECTIVE SOCIETIES

Since it is complicated to manage and collect royalties, there are collective societies that exist to help third parties manage their royalties, including SODRAC, ASCAP, BMI, SOCAM and CMRRA. All of these groups are important resources for those who want to register their music rights or license rights of others.

CONCLUSION

If you want to incorporate someone else's work, which is subject to royalty, into your own work, you need permission. You may need to sign release forms, pay royalties, and get written permission. You should have a checklist and make sure you retain a file with all the releases and other contracts connected to your project. When dealing with minors, you must get releases from their parent or legal guardian.

BUSINESS MODELS AND OTHER LEGAL ISSUES

There are three main ways a person can conduct his business.

SOLE PROPRIETORSHIP

An individual can conduct business as a sole proprietorship. In this case, a person may register a business name at the Registraire des entreprises. Please note, a registered business name is a trade name under which a person carries on his trade or business, it does not constitute a company. For example, Jane Doe is a graphic designer doing business as Jane Design or Jane Communications. This tells the world that this is the name that Jane does business under, but Jane remains personally liable for the business. She may use her name on a business card but she must sign contracts in her personal name. Similarly if Frank does business with Jane, Frank needs to know her complete name and address because if there is any problem Frank needs to go after Jane personally.

If you do business as a sole proprietorship, *you* are the business, and therefore the contracts you sign in your name make you personally liable.

PARTNERSHIP

Another business model is the "partnership." This is when you and a friend go into business together. In a general partnership, the partners share the profits and losses. They are liable personally for the acts of the partnership. It is important to know whom you get into business with and what the contribution and responsibility of each partner is. It is advisable to have an agreement that sets out some basic terms such as what each partner expects of the other partner and what happens upon death, disability, or dispute. Who will own the assets of the partnership, etc.? Like a sole proprietorship, a partnership in Quebec must have a name and needs to be registered with the Registraire des entreprises. Be careful when you enter these relationships. You can be held personally liable for the acts of your partner and have to pay for them even if you are not at fault personally.

CORPORATION OR COMPANY

A company is called a "moral person" in law, therefore it is a separate entity from you. Since it is a separate entity, it has separate legal obligations. The owner of the company is called a shareholder. The company is run by its directors and officers. In Quebec, the company must be registered with the Registraire des entreprises. If it is a Canada business corporation, it must also file annual returns with Industry Canada. The important thing to remember about a corporation is that, legally, it is a separate person, therefore, you will not be personally liable for the acts of the corporation except in limited circumstances. It is also important when you sign a contract that you sign in the name of the corporation and not in your own name. For example: "ABC Inc. per:

Jane Doe." That way you know whom you are contracting with and you are engaging the right party. You may have to assign your Intellectual Property rights to your own corporation if you want the corporation to own them. The corporation must file its own tax returns and has its own obligations. If more than one person owns the corporation, i.e., there is more than one shareholder, it is useful to have a shareholder agreement to set out roles and responsibilities. For example, who can sign at the bank and for what amounts. What happens if one shareholder wants to sell his share; what happens if he dies or is disabled. Who will be responsible for financing the business? These are just a few points to discuss.

SIGNING CONTRACTS

Many artists are asked to sign agreements, which give another person the right to use their work. It is important that you understand the documents you sign. If you have given something up you may not be able to regain, make sure you understand what you are giving up. Be clear about what you are signing and how long the agreement will last. Also, make sure that you are protecting yourself and that you are not giving away rights which are not yours to give.

In addition to getting appropriate accounting advice to deal with taxes and record keeping, etc, there are things to keep in mind when contracting with other people.

Often people say they have a "handshake" deal. Although it is possible to have oral agreements, they are much more difficult to enforce. Traditionally, important agreements should be set down in writing. Even if not all of the terms have been negotiated or agreed upon, as long as there are certain key elements that have been agreed upon, there could be a binding agreement against the parties. This means the parties can enforce their obligations against one another.

What do you need to know?: You need to know whom you are doing business with. Is it a company? Is it a person? Is it a partnership? Make sure you get the full name. A full name of a corporation or company should include "Inc." or "Ltd." It is not enough just to have half a name of the company, because if you must take action, it may not be possible to sue that person.

Make sure the key elements of the contracts are set down in writing, even if it is only a letter of agreement. What are key contract terms? For example, why do we have a contract? Is it to sell something, to assign something, to perform something? What are the terms? What is the length of the contract? How much money do you get paid? When do you get paid? What do you get paid? When does the contract begin? When does the contract end? What happens if the contract doesn't work out or if there is disagreement?

When do you have a contract?: A legally binding contract must have three key elements:

The parties to the contract must have the capacity to enter into the contract. For example, a contract entered into with a minor child is probably not binding if the child's parent or guardian did not enter into the contract.

The parties to the contract have to agree on the contract and its terms. Generally the contract should set out its purpose and the key elements, such as time, price, obligations of the parties, deliverables, etc. The contract is formed when and where acceptances are received.

Until the terms have been agreed upon, the parties may just be proposing offers to contract and counter offers.

Contracts can be freely negotiated between the parties. Sometimes one party settles the key terms and the other party signs the contract with out negotiating this. This is known as an adhesion contract. Adhesion contracts are interpreted in favour of the person who signs it and against the person who drafted it.

Be careful and make sure you know whom you are dealing with and whether or not that person has the authority to enter into the contract. Make sure that everything that is important to you is set in that contract before you sign it. If something isn't there, you may want to include a sentence which states that it is an initial agreement to govern your relationship until such time as you enter a long form agreement with standard terms and conditions.

THINGS TO CONSIDER WHEN CONTRACTING - THE BOILER PLATE

Most sophisticated contracts may include some terms and conditions which you do not understand or may not be aware of. For example, here are some that you may want to consider.

A. REPRESENTATIONS AND WARRANTIES

Many contracts require that you represent and warrant certain things. These are statements that you are making to the effect that you have the rights and capacity to do what you are promising to under the contract. If the work you are licensing is a multi-media work or a film or a composite work, you are also probably representing and warranting that you also have the rights of the third parties you use in your work to license. That is why it is very important whenever you start any multi-media project that you keep very good records, which includes a record of permission to use or sell the work. All your releases for your location, for your artist, for works, should be kept in one specific binder. It is an easy way to do business so that you know if there is any question, you have names and addresses of the various individuals. This is also important because if you need to get insurance for errors and omissions, (which is sometimes required when you broadcast the work), you will be able to help your lawyer in validating the fact that you do have all the proper releases you need.

B. INDEMNITY

If you agree to indemnify someone, you may have to compensate that person for any loss they may suffer as a result of your actions.

C. LIMITATION OF LIABILITY

In certain cases, the parties will seek to limit their liability to a fixed amount or to direct damages. If you agree to indemnify someone for a loss or harm, you should try to set limits on what you will be responsible for.

D. ARBITRATION

Arbitration is a dispute resolution mechanism. In arbitration, instead of going before a judge or a Court, you go before an arbitrator, a specialist in dispute resolution, to help resolve the issue.

These technical legal questions generally should be discussed with an attorney so that you properly understand them. Some of you will belong to certain associations which will have mandatory obligations or standard form contracts and you can contact your association to get more information on that.

TIPS ON CONTRACTS

It is important to know the key requirements for your industry and for your art. If you visit the websites listed in the resource section, you will see many references to some standard form agreements that are commonly used. For example, you can look at the Canadian Writers' Guild Agreement.

TAXES

It is important when you negotiate your rate, to ascertain whether the other party is withholding taxes i.e., what is the amount you get in your pocket after the deal is done? There could be sales tax and/or withholding tax. It is important to get your financial advisors to inform you about consequences of your earnings from a tax perspective.

RECORD KEEPING

It is important to keep a record of your discussions when you are dealing with people. Although it may sound obvious, you should create a separate file for every contract or project you enter into. Keep a copy of the contract and the drafts and notes you have made. Although generally, they may not be admissible if the matter goes to Court, they may be helpful as a reminder to you, as to why certain clauses were negotiated or what you had agreed to do (your intention). They could also be useful for subsequent transactions.

If it is your work that you are licensing, it is worthwhile that you invest some time and money to get a proper licensing agreement in place to use when licensing to others. Larger organizations may have standard form agreements that they want you to sign. In that case, you should take a look at your own contract and see where your contract differs from theirs. You may not be able to successfully have them change all the terms of their agreement to yours, but at the very least, you will know what changes have been made.

Generally, large organizations that deal internationally may have certain standards that they need to apply because of their operation, and they may take more rights to protect themselves.

BIBLIOGRAPHY

LEGISLATION

Copyright Act, R.S.C. 1985, c. C-42

Trademarks Act, R.S.C. 1985, c. T-13

Trademarks Regulations, SOR/96-195

Civil Code of Quebec, S.Q. 1991, c-64 (Legal Persons : art. 298-364; Partnerships :

Art. 2186-2279; Employment Contracts : art. 2085-2097; Personality Rights : art. 1-9)

An Act Respecting the Legal Publicity of Sole Proprietorships, Partnerships and

Legal Persons, S.Q. 1993, c-48

Companies Act, R.S.Q., c. C-38

Canada Business Corporations Act, R.S.C. 1985, c. C-44

Industrial Design Act, R.S.C. 1985, c.-19

Industrial Design Regulations, SOR/99-460

Charter of Human Rights and Freedoms, R.S.Q., c. C-12

An Act Respecting the Professional Status of Engagement of Performing, Recording and Film Artists, R.S.Q., c. S-32.1

An Act Respecting the Professional Status of Artists, Individual Art, Arts and Craft and Literature and Their Contracts with Promoters, R.S.Q., c.S-32.01

ACCOUNTING FOR ARTISTS

Artists and other entrepreneurs in creative fields often view accounting, taxation, and bookkeeping as foreign intrusions into their real work. After all, taxes bring angst, while art brings pleasure.

Nonetheless, if you want to be a self-sufficient self-employed artist, you need to be aware of some accountancy issues so that you don't get in trouble with the government.

In this section, we provide some basic accounting pointers to help you get started, including several tips that can help you save money and taxes and make even greater profits.

Here are some key words you'll come across in accounting and bookkeeping:

Deductibility: Generally, a business is allowed to deduct expenses incurred in the course of earning taxable income

Assets: Assets are things—both tangible and intangible—that you own and amounts owed to you for goods sold or services rendered (usually referred to as "accounts receivable")

Liabilities: Debts, monies you owe

Revenue: Money coming to you for goods sold or services rendered. Also "non-earned" money like dividends, interest payments and arts grants

Expenses: Money spent in the course of operating a business

FAQS FOR THE SELF-EMPLOYED ARTIST

Below are several frequently asked questions related to the financial needs and obligations of the self-employed artist. Note that the information below in no way replaces the professional advice of an accountant, bookkeeper, or business consultant. In fact, we recommend that you speak to an accounting professional who is familiar with the needs of self-employed entrepreneurs.

1. How do I get started?

Keep track of all the money coming into your account (this is your revenue), whether through sales or financial grants, AND all the money going out to pay for business-related expenses and assets (see below for what counts as a business-related expense).

Monthly filing system
If you are well-organized, you will want to develop a monthly filing system whereby you will table your revenue and expenses each month and attach all invoices and receipts.

Shoebox Method
If you are overwhelmed at the thought of doing your own bookkeeping, start by using the shoebox method: keep all receipts together in one envelope and all invoices in another. Store these in a box so that they are accessible at tax time.

2. Why do I need to keep track of my revenue and expenses?

Every April, Canadians must file an income tax return with the federal Canada Revenue Agency. Residents of Quebec must also file a separate but similar return with Revenu Québec.

Both tax agencies want to know how much money you earned during the past year, and other important facts including:

- Are you married?

- Do you have children? If so, how many?

- Do you have any other dependents?

- Did you attend school over the course of the year?

- Did you make charitable donations?

- Have you received any money other than through employment?

Based on your answers to these and other questions, the tax agencies determine whether you owe them income tax or whether you overpaid and are eligible for a tax refund. The latter case usually only applies to people working as employees with deductions at source.

It is very important for entrepreneurs and self-employed artists to keep track of their business-related expenses throughout the year.

Expenses you can claim from business or professional activities will reduce your net income. It is a good idea to claim expenses because the lower your income, the less income tax you have to pay.

- For instance, say you sold four canvases last year, each for $25,000 (we can dream, can't we?). With an annual income of $100,000, you'd find yourself in a very high tax bracket.

- But suppose it cost you $15,000 to pay for materials, transportation, and advanced oil painting technique classes for each of the four canvases. That means that you spent $60,000 on business-related expenses.

- Then add the $12,000 a year you pay to rent your studio.
- And don't forget to add the $3,000 spent producing marketing materials during the year, including your website, business cards, professional portfolio and press kit, which is how you got noticed in the first place and why you've had a steady stream of sales.

Revenue: 4 canvases sold @ $25,000	= $100,000
minus cost of materials, etc. per canvas: $15,000	- $60,000
minus monthly rent for studio: $1,000	- $12,000
minus cost of marketing materials: $3,000	-$3,000
Your actual (net) income at the end of the year:	= $25,000

- After you've factored in all your expenses, your income is quite a bit less than what you earned.

By recording your work-related expenses, you'll be able to prove to the government that your real (or net) income is $25,000—not the gross $100,000. And your income taxes will be greatly reduced.

3. What kinds of things count as business-related expenses?

In short, you deduct expenses that you incur while earning or trying to earn income. The rules for deductible expenses are laid out in the Tax Act, but for a far less convoluted explanation, read the booklet that comes with your tax returns.

Below are some of the types of expenses you'll likely incur as a self-employed artist.

NOTE that credit card statements are not sufficient proof of expenses. Keep all your original receipts.

Workspace rent or interest on mortgage payments, plus other related costs, like utilities.
Even if you work out of your house or apartment, you can claim a portion of your monthly rent or the interest on your mortgage payment, plus utilities, *as an expense.*

For example, imagine that you have a 1,000 square foot apartment, and you use one room measuring 150 square feet as a studio.

How much of your apartment can you deduct as an allowable business expense? Here's the formula:

$$150 / 1000 \times 100 = 15\%$$

(The proportion is generally calculated by floor space.)

So, in this example, 15 per cent of your home expenses can be claimed as business expenses.

This percentage applies to the cost of electricity, heating, rent, mortgage interest, and repairs and maintenance.

Costs related to transportation
If you own or lease a vehicle, be sure to keep track of your mileage for business-related excursions. You are allowed to deduct a portion of you car costs as legitimate business expenses.

For example, imagine that you put 30,000 km on your odometer in a year. Of that, 10,000 km were business-related excursions (visits with clients, travel to an arts festival in the Eastern Townships).

How much of your car can you deduct as an allowable business expense? Here's the formula:

$$10,000 \text{ business km} / 30,000 \text{ total km} \times 100 = 33.33\%$$

So, in this example, 33.33 per cent of your total car costs can be deducted as legitimate business expenses.

This includes things like gas, insurance, registration, license fees, lease payments*, parking space rental/parking meters, interest paid on finance loans, repairs and maintenance, and car washes.

In 2003, the government capped the allowable lease expense at $800 a month. Check with an accountant to discover the maximum allowable lease expense for your car payments.

If you don't own a car but use public transportation or taxis, these costs can be expenses too.

Entertaining clients and potential clients
At the federal level, you are allowed to claim 50 per cent of the cost of business lunches (or dinners or breakfasts) at which you treated a work-related colleague. The deductibility rate is lower at the provincial level.

Keep your receipts and write the name of the client on the back of each receipt.

You can also claim some of the costs for organizing an event such as a catered vernissage, book launch, or business Christmas party.

Marketing and self-promotion costs

Any money disbursed to market, promote or advertise your products and services are allowable business expenses.

These include:

- Costs of creating and maintaining a promotional website (including domain name registration, web hosting and hiring a professional web designer to create the site);

- Costs to design and print business cards, press kits and folders, and other promotional materials;

- Costs associated with throwing promotional events, like a comedy night, piano recital, poetry reading, etc.;

- Any advertising costs incurred throughout the year.

Office rental and supplies

As mentioned above, you can claim your monthly work space rent payment or the interest on your mortgage payments, or a proportion of your home rent or mortgage interest if you work from home.

You can also deduct costs like:

- Office supplies (pens, staplers, etc.)

- Paper, stationery, envelopes

- Office equipment (phone, fax machine)

- Telephone line and long distance charges, Internet connection, cellular phone

Cost of other materials

Here you can deduct all the specialized tools you need to practice your trade. These might include:

- Paint brushes	- Paint
- Canvases	- Sheet music
- Fabric	- Sewing machine
- Computer software	- Costumes
- Make-up	- Wardrobe

Note: Purchases of items that last longer than a year cannot be claimed as business expenses, but they can be written off against your income over their useful lifetime. This is known as depreciation, which is defined as "the allocation of the cost of the asset over the useful life of the asset".

For example, if you go through several pairs of ballet shoes, paintbrushes, or knitting needles over the course of a year, you can legitimately claim these as expenses. However if you purchase a car, a computer, or an expensive drawing table for your business that will last longer than a year, you claim the depreciation on the purchase over the next several years.

Travel expenses
In general, if you have to travel for work related purposes, then you can claim transportation costs, hotels, and meals.

- If you are a comic artist headed to the comic festival in Angoulême, France to meet with publishers and bookstore owners, your travel costs would probably be considered legitimate expenses.
- If your band is heading to Victoriaville, Quebec to perform at the Festival International de Musique Actuelle, your travel costs would probably be considered legitimate expenses.
- If you take an "inspirational" trip to Club Med, Bora Bora in advance of the launch of your Fall fashion collection, there's a good chance you will not be permitted to claim these costs as legitimate business expenses.

Association fees and dues
You can usually deduct the fees paid to belong to a professional association, guild, or trade union.

Training and development/ education
You can deduct the cost of courses or classes taken during the year if they are related to updating and improving your skills. You cannot claim courses or classes as expenses if the subject matter is unrelated to your declared trade or leads toward another career.

You can also claim the costs of relevant magazine subscriptions or book purchases.

For instance:

- A journalist could probably deduct course fees for a photography class taken during the year (if it is likely that the photography skills gained will improve income earning potential).
- A filmmaker could probably deduct the cost of a subscription to Qui Fait Quoi magazine as well as the cost of purchasing *Feature Film Making for Dummies* and *Filmmaking at Used-Car Prices.*

On the other hand, it is *unlikely* that:

- A fashion designer could deduct the cost of a creative writing course.

- A photographer could deduct the cost of a subscription to *New Yorker* magazine.

- A graphic designer could deduct the cost of joining the Quebec Theatre Federation.

There may be additional deductions that are applicable to your particular line of work. Consult with a professional association, the tax office, or an accountant familiar with the needs of self-employed artists, entrepreneurs, or small business owners.

Also, keep in mind that different tax forms are available from Revenue Canada for artists in different lines of work.

- Performing arts: 525-R

- Visual artists and writers: 504-R2

- Dispositions of Cultural Property to Designated Canadian Institutions: 407-R4.

Check with the tax office for a tax form specific to your line of work.

4. I only use top-of-the-line, very expensive materials for my work. Can I deduct the full cost of my materials or only the cost of average-priced materials?

The taxman expects your expenses to be reasonable and relevant. For example, you'll have a very tough time convincing the taxman that you need to drive a Ferrari instead of a Ford. When it comes to the specific tools and materials of your trade, the situation is a little less clear, but you'd better be able to justify your expenses.

5. I've received a grant to complete a project. Is this considered income? Do I have to pay taxes on it?

Yes and yes. Grant money is taxable, and taxes are not withheld by the granting agency. Therefore, make sure you put a portion of the grant money aside for tax time.

6. It's been two years since I've filed taxes. What do I do? Am I in trouble with the law?

There is no penalty for filing your tax return after the deadline if you don't owe anything. On the other hand, if you do owe back taxes, they charge interest for every day you're late, and a late-filing penalty on top of that. Don't let your taxes get away from you! If the process is overwhelming, don't hesitate to get help from an accounting or tax-preparation professional, even if it costs money. It'll end up costing far less than the penalties.

7. I've been in business for five years and I've had five straight years of loss. I'll probably have losses again this year. What will happen? Will I be audited?

FACT: Nine out of ten small businesses lose money in their first few years of operation. However, if you keep losing money over longer periods, you'll probably be asked to prove that you're running a business and not just a hobby.

In order to claim business expenses, there needs to be a reasonable expectation of profit. No one goes into business to perpetually lose money. After six or seven years of ongoing losses, the government may want to meet with you in person to assess your taxes.

If you can't prove that you have a reasonable expectation of earning income from your work, then it will be considered a hobby, and your expenses will no longer be deductible from your other income. In fact, it's even possible that the government will force you to pay back taxes.

8. Do I need to hire an accountant? How much will this cost me?

Accountants charge by the hour, so a more complicated tax return will take more time to complete and will cost more. Depending on the accountant and the complexity of your business, it could cost anywhere from $50 to several hundred dollars. Larger businesses can expect to pay much more. Although an accountant isn't strictly necessary in many cases, they are experts at doing taxes.

Doing your own tax returns by hand is time-consuming, especially if you're self-employed, but it's certainly possible. There are several easy-to-use tax preparation applications for both Mac and PC computers that walk you through every line of the tax return. These applications usually cost in the neighbourhood of $35.

While you don't need to be a tax expert to complete a tax return by yourself, the chances of making mistakes are much greater. This might delay your tax refund, or even reduce the amount you're entitled to.

It's a good idea to get the tax forms and tax guides from post offices during tax time, February to April. You can also download them in PDF form directly from the Canada Revenue Agency and Revenu Québec websites.

- Canada Revenue Agency:
  www.cra-arc.gc.ca

- Revenu Québec
www.revenu.gouv.qc.ca/eng/ministere/index.asp

OTHER CONSIDERATIONS:

If any of the following apply to you, then you must register for a federal and provincial business number (which can be done at each government's tax office):

- You have sales above $30,000 a year

- You are incorporated

- You do import/ export

- You employ others and pay them
www.businessregistration-
inscriptionentreprise.gc.ca/dchmf/brom/bro/about-e.html
(Tel: Fed: 1-800-267-1267. Quebec: 514-864-6299.)

If you employ at least one full-time or part-time employee, you must:

• Register with Revenu Québec for a Quebec Sales Tax (TVQ) and Goods and Services Tax (GST) number
www.mrq.gouv.qc.ca/eng/travailleur_autonome/affaires/premier
es_demarches/immatricul.asp

• Register with the Commission de la santé et de la sécurité du travail (CSST) and make regular contributions. www.csst.qc.ca

(Source: www.infoentrepreneurs.org/english)

HOW TO PRICE YOUR WORK

Some artists feel that their work is too important to be sold for profit, and have accepted the opportunity costs of their convictions.

This book is for the rest of you.

In this chapter, we provide tips on pricing your work so that, at the end of the day, you will have earned more from your creation than what you put into it.

IMPORTANT DEFINITIONS:

Fixed costs:
Costs that are independent of any particular project, that is, any expense you incur, whether or not you produce any work. Examples include:

- **Indirect labour costs:** Fees paid for administrative services (i.e.: your accountant)

- **Overhead costs:** Costs that are not directly related to the project but are required to run your business, including studio or office rental, utilities, advertising and promotion, professional membership fees, insurance, etc.

Variable costs
Costs that are dependent on a particular project, and vary with the level of production. Examples include:

- **Direct labour costs:** Price per hour you charge for yourself, or the hourly wage you pay your employee for the project in question.

- **Raw materials:** Materials used in the production of a particular project. These include paint, fabric, buttons, beads, string, paper, laser-printer toner, etc.

Sales:
Revenue derived from selling your products or services. This does not include grant money, dividends or interest payments.

BREAK-EVEN POINT

The first step in establishing your pricing strategy is to determine the price at which you need to sell your art in order to break even.

Here is a formula to determine your break-even point:

VARIABLE COSTS + FIXED COSTS = SALES

(Raw materials + labour costs)

+

(Overhead costs + other fixed costs)

=

(The price at which you sold the piece of work)

Let's look at an example for a painter. Assume each painting created during the year was about the same size and required the same amount of materials and labour.

VARIABLE COSTS

The cost of her paint and canvas per painting is:	$150
Consider the number of hours worked	$225
per canvas and an hourly wage that is fair.	
(15 hours spent working @ $15/hour)	

Say she painted 20 canvases last year

Total variable costs are	
20 canvases x ($150 + $225)	$7,500

FIXED COSTS

Now add her fixed costs for the year.	+$2,000
The cost to paint 20 canvases last year was:	$9,500

TO BREAK EVEN, SHE SHOULD SELL EACH CANVAS AT:

(Variable costs + fixed costs) ÷	
(Number of canvases produced)	
$9,500 ÷ 20 canvases	= $475

Since each canvas cost her $475 to produce, by selling them at that price, she would earn back everything she spent to create them. But, she still isn't making any money.

EARNING A PROFIT

One way to determine how much you must charge to make a profit is to decide how much profit you want to make.

Say our painter has set a goal of earning $5,000 over and above her costs.

Target profit: $5,000

We know that her costs per canvas are:

(Variable costs + Fixed costs) / #Number of canvases

$9,500 ÷ 20 = $475

If she wants to make a profit of $5,000, then she must add that number in to her total costs.

(Variable costs + Fixed costs + **Target profit**) ÷ 20

($9,500 + **$5,000**) ÷ 20

= $725

So, if she sold 20 canvases at $725 instead of $475, she would make a profit of $5,000 at the end of the year. If her selling price was less than $725, she'd make less profit. If she sold her canvasses at less than $475 a piece, she'd be losing money.

SMART PRICING

It is important to keep your prices in line with similar offerings on the market in order to stay competitive and be taken seriously in the marketplace.

- A fashion designer should visit target stores before bringing in a collection to see what kind of price points they carry. If you price your work too high or too low, the buyer will know you haven't done your research and you'll lose credibility.

- Freelance writers should visit www.writers.ca, a resource website owned by the Periodical Writers Association of Canada (PWAC). There you'll find a rate table with suggested rates for different types of writing projects.

- Graphic designers, painters, photographers and other artists should inquire with peers and with professional associations about pricing strategies.

- Unions and professional associations usually have information about industry standards.

WHAT ARE SOME OF THE FIRST THINGS A SELF-EMPLOYED ARTIST CAN DO TO CUT COSTS AND IMPROVE PROFITS?

- Choose a lower rent location for their studio or office, or work at home.

- Obtain products, services, and work materials through co-ops or barter programs.

- Charge more per hour, if the market determines that this is reasonable.

- Work fewer hours, subcontract part of the work to someone who can do it for less money or hire an assistant who works for a lower wage than you.

Lastly, don't undervalue your work. This is your livelihood, your career. This is what you do to put food on your table. You work just as hard as a lawyer or a doctor or a metalworker, and you're entitled to a fair return on your effort. It's fine to volunteer when you're just getting acquainted with your milieu, and in most cases, doing so will help launch your career. However, you have to know when to start charging what you are worth. If your writing is good enough to be published, your photos good enough to be printed, then you are good enough to be paid.

LESSONS FROM THE REAL WORLD

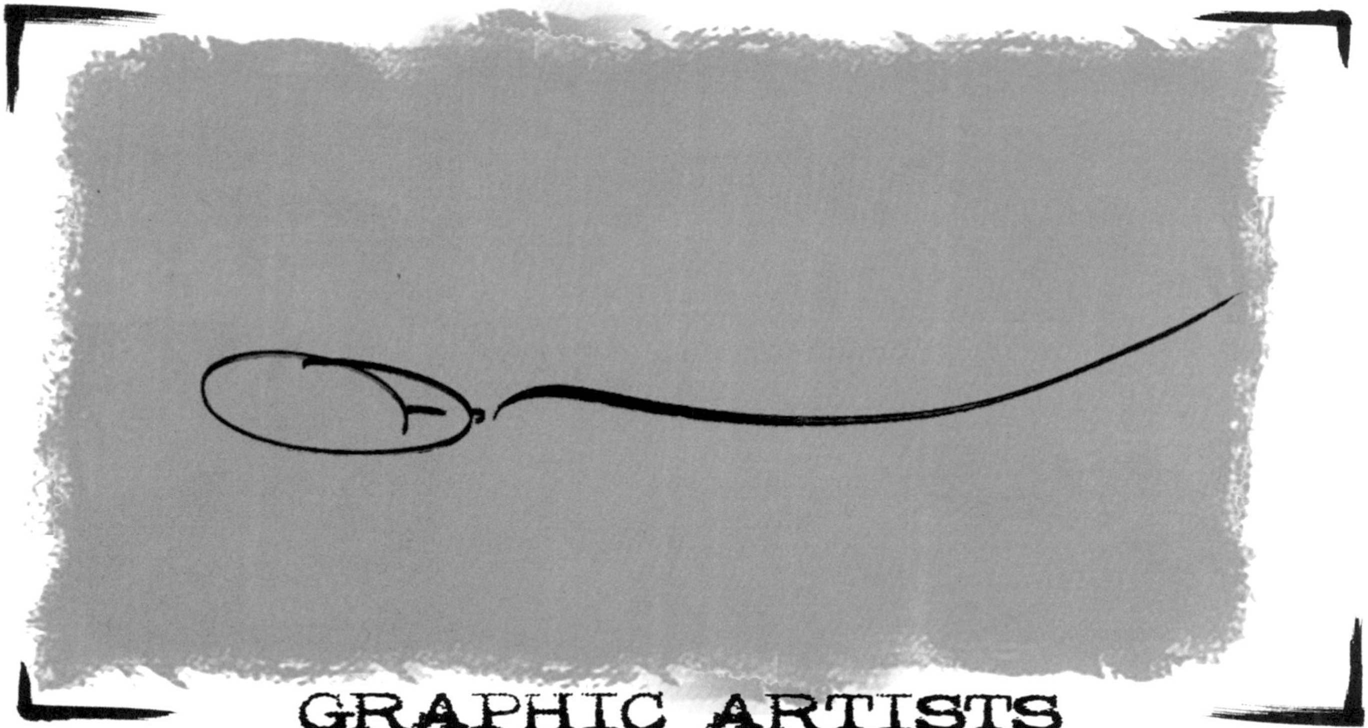

GRAPHIC ARTISTS

"Dive in. Biting off more than you can chew is always better than taking baby steps." - Andrew Elvish, Softimage Creative Director

So you wanna be A GRAPHIC ARTIST?

"I only buy it for the ads," you whisper in embarrassment when your significant other catches you flipping through that notorious glossy magazine. You know the one we mean.

No need to sweat your secret pleasures here. We believe you. As an aspiring graphic artist, your passion is less in the message than in the medium, right? And we're not just talking about magazine ads, either! The graphic arts encompass a universe of design possibilities: creating book covers, designing computer game characters or websites, even inventing new fonts.

In this section, we feature the perspectives of four Montrealers employed in the graphic arts, all with unique talents, visions and jobs.

If you recognize yourself in the expert advice offered in this section, or if it leaves you feeling a little unsure about a career in graphic art, you may want to further investigate the following related occupations:

- Creative designers and craftspersons
- Photographers
- Graphics arts technicians and technical and co-ordinating occupations in motion pictures, broadcasting and the performing arts

(Source: National Occupation Classification, published by Human Resources Development Canada)

PANEL OF GRAPHIC ARTISTS

In this section, we interviewed:

DENIS DULUDE
Graphic Designer and Co-founder, 2Rebels Font Foundry

ANDREW ELVISH
Creative Director, Softimage

TOM KOURI
President, High Touch Communications Inc.

RACHEL STEPHAN
President and Graphic Designer, Les sens créatifs inc.

SCHOOL

According to the National Occupational Classification (NOC), about one in four aspiring graphic designers has an undergraduate university degree in visual arts with a specialization in graphic design, commercial art, graphic communications or cartooning, or a college or other degree in graphic design.

Our panel of experts is divided about whether a degree is necessary to make it as a graphic designer. Two of the four experts on our panel have formal training, the third got into the business after taking a night course (but now teaches at the university level) and the fourth is entirely self-taught. Though the jury is divided about the necessity of formal education, all of our experts stressed the importance of staying up-to-date with the latest technologies to remain competitive in the field.

Rachel Stephan, the graphic artist responsible for this very book, said she learned two important skills at school that allowed her to take her talent to the business world: working within a structure and working within guidelines.

Read on for more thoughts on the topic:

- **LEARN TO DESIGN WITH PURPOSE**
  Rachel Stephan: "At school, I learned to design with a purpose, rather than just designing something a certain way because it looked pretty. In this business, designs are meant to sell; there has to be a marketing strategy behind your art. School is a good place to learn about this aspect of design."

- **A DIPLOMA SHOWS THAT YOU'RE SERIOUS ABOUT MAKING IT**
  Tom Kouri: "School is important, there's no doubt about it. It indicates that you have discipline and an ability to move towards a goal."

- THERE ARE THINGS TO BE LEARNED BOTH IN SCHOOL AND ON YOUR OWN

Denis Dulude: "I teach typography at UQAM. From this experience, I have come to realize that students learn a ton of things in university that they would not touch upon if they were learning the craft on their own. The structure of a graphic design program makes the overall learning process a bit easier.

"That said, I think learning on your own teaches you other great skills, like being independent and self-motivated. You also become skilled at making do with available resources. I think that if you're passionate about design but don't have the means to get to school, you'll find a way to make it in the business."

- GRADUATES TEND TO EXCEL IN A SPECIFIC AREA; INDEPENDENT LEARNERS TEND TO HAVE BROAD-BASED SKILLS

Andrew Elvish: "There are a lot of benefits to going to school, but there are also some disadvantages. For instance, some graduates will be very specialized and will not be able to grow in all sorts of directions, whereas designers who just jump into the business tend to be more versatile."

PORTFOLIO

Our panel of experts was unanimous: you can't get a foot in the door without a good portfolio under your arm.

Below, we've listed their most helpful tips:

- TAKE THE 'LESS IS MORE' APPROACH

The object of a portfolio isn't to show how prolific you've been, but to show how creative and professional you can be.

"Many emerging designers overcrowd their portfolios with everything they have ever done," says Denis Dulude. "When this is the case, there isn't enough to show from any one field, or mediocre work is included. It is better to have less work, but only great work."

- SHOW A VARIETY OF YOUR BEST WORK

Unless you are applying for a highly specialized position, Rachel Stephan recommends including a broad sampling of your work.

She suggests putting examples of the following in your portfolio:

- Logos and corporate identity designs
- Brochures
- Posters
- Pamphlets

Tom Kouri suggests that you show off both print and web-based designs to show that you can work in the new economy.

SHOW ONLY YOUR VERY BEST WORK

"Quality is more important that quantity," says Denis Dulude, and cautions, "If you're hesitating about whether to include a piece because you aren't quite sure that it's your best work, but it would be your only example of a logo, for instance, don't include it."

SHOW PROJECTS THAT WILL RESONATE WITH THE POTENTIAL EMPLOYER

"You cannot have just one portfolio and use it at every interview or for every pitch you make," says Rachel Stephan. "Your portfolio has to be tailored to and personalized for every company you approach."

Andrew Elvish suggests that you show a prospective employer that you can meet and exceed their expectations by carefully choosing the projects included in your portfolio.

"Show them a project that was finished on a really tight deadline," he says, "or show one that was completed on a really small budget."

SAVE YOUR MOST IMPRESSIVE PIECES FOR THE BEGINNING AND THE END OF YOUR PORTFOLIO

Rachel Stephan says showing off your portfolio is like writing a story. "You need to get their attention from the outset, like you would with a title, and you need to finish off with a bang. First impressions are important, and the last thing they see is what they'll remember the most vividly."

PUT YOUR WORK ONLINE

Andrew Elvish says any up-and-coming designer should have their work displayed on a professionally designed, easily navigated website.

OTHER WORDS OF WISDOM

Tom Kouri thinks emerging designers should include samples of any typographical work they may have done. "Type is the largest component of communication, and this is what we are in, the communication business," he says.

Also, says Kouri, "if you have any natural, artistic ability as an illustrator, you'll want to show that off too."

"Don't be self-conscious about your vision and don't be afraid to share your ideas. If you are always hesitant and unsure, it makes you look like you don't know what you're doing." -
Andrew Elvish

GETTING STARTED

After reading through the previous section, the idea of compiling an impressive portfolio may seem overwhelming. Relax, your future employers and prospective clients know where you're coming from. Each of the successful graphic designers we interviewed told us they started in the same place: the bottom.

Our panel of designers is unanimous: a good portfolio along with an internship is the best way to get started in this business. And, while nobody expects you to produce pieces of Picasso-esque genius yet, they do expect you to come in with a great attitude and a willingness to learn as you go.

Here, in their own words, is what our panel told us about landing an internship or an entry-level position and making it work:

- **EVERYONE STARTS AT THE BOTTOM. MAKE THE MOST OF IT AND WATCH YOURSELF MOVE UP THE LADDER FAST**

    Andrew Elvish: "Find a company that you would like to work for, and, if you can't immediately land the job you want, apply to be a receptionist. Answering the phones wasn't my favourite thing, but I got my foot in the door that way."

    Rachel Stephan: "Some people aren't willing to climb the ladder. They want to start at the top. You have to be willing to start small. Whatever it is, it's a foot in the door. From there, show them what you can do. If you're good, you'll move up very quickly."

- **KNOW WHERE YOU WANT TO GO WITH YOUR CAREER**

    Andrew Elvish: "It's really important to be able to look ahead in your field and see that there are opportunities available. In any field, you have to know where you are headed; you should be able to look ahead at least five years. Set goals for yourself; they will drive you and move you forward."

    Denis Dulude: "If you feel that you want to manage a business, go the freelance route. But if you want to focus solely on design or gain experience on big accounts, apply to work at a design studio."

- **RESEARCH POTENTIAL EMPLOYERS**

    Denis Dulude: "If you decide you want to work at a design studio, it is important to shop around and apply to companies where you think your design style would fit in. For instance, don't apply at a studio renowned for very straight-forward, classic designs if your style is very cutting-edge."

BE DETERMINED AND FOLLOW UP

Tom Kouri: "I get a lot of resumes from people who don't follow up. If you really want a job, you should always follow up.

"Also, it's important you do your research. Go to the company's website and read about them. Make sure you spell the company name correctly when you apply. Know what kinds of designs they've worked on. Familiarize yourself with their completed projects."

VOLUNTEER

Rachel Stephan: "People in a position to hire young graphic designers will only look briefly at work produced in school. When you are just getting started, consider volunteering your services. This will help you build up your portfolio by giving you pieces from the real world."

INTERNING ALLOWS YOU TO TEST THE WATERS

Rachel Stephan: "Interning gives emerging designers a chance to see if they like a certain company or a specific job. It also allows them to learn and grow without the pressure of being an employee; it is understood that interns are there to learn."

PUT YOURSELF OUT THERE

Andrew Elvish: "Some designers think that people should come to them because they're obviously talented individuals. In reality, you have to be very aggressive when you're looking to secure a contract. It's about going out there and saying 'you've got to use me because I'm better' or 'I offer better services' or 'I offer more competitive prices' without being hard-edged about it."

Denis Dulude: "Don't be afraid to say 'I don't have experience, but I know what you, the customer, need. Let me show you what I can do.'

NETWORK

Andrew Elvish: "[For me, networking] was about going out to parties and striking up a conversation with someone I knew was in a position to hire freelancers. Or, if I had heard about someone from a friend that was looking to hire, I'd give them a call and say 'I know you're looking, and this is what I can do for you.'"

Tom Kouri: "There are many groups and associations that emerging designers should join. Many times, they have discount rates if you're a student, so join and gain visibility. Go to the conferences or luncheons and meet people."

Rachel Stephan: "Joining a specific association was part of my marketing strategy. I wanted to meet people and create personal contacts, and becoming a member of industry associations is a good way to do this.

"It's also important to be active within the association that you join. For example, I often sponsor events that the association I am a member of runs or I sit on committees. This way, my company logo is everywhere."

EARLY IN YOUR CAREER, EVERY JOB IS AS MUCH FOR YOUR OWN PORTFOLIO AS IT IS FOR THE CLIENT

Andrew Elvish: "In the early stages of your career, you have to accept that you aren't going to bill clients for every hour worked. You have to say to yourself 'I am taking this job because I want it for my portfolio or because I want to include this specific company on my resume.'"

COMPUTER SKILLS ARE FUNDAMENTAL

Andrew Elvish: "Good graphic designers aren't just comfortable with computers; they are able to operate them on a very fundamental level. You have to know the PC and Mac platforms and you should be able to install programs and fix your computer. Also, you have to become proficient in all the tools of your trade. The core tools, to me, are QuarkXpress, Photoshop, and Illustrator.

"If you are a print designer, you should also have some understanding of interactive and web design. If web design is a black hole to you, you'll be forced to pass on your work to the web designer and hope that they stick to your design. If you have a certain understanding of it, you will be able to give your input; it will be a collaborative effort."

START AN E-MAIL MARKETING CAMPAIGN

Tom Kouri: "As you network, build up a list of contacts. Now and again, send them e-mails with news about new projects you are working on along with links to samples on your website."

UNDERSTAND THAT THIS ISN'T A 9-5 JOB

Andrew Elvish: "Don't come in to a design studio expecting to work banker's hours. Design should be more of a vocation than a job. You have to be passionate about it, and sometimes that means working late to get your design just right."

THINK BEFORE YOU SPEAK

Andrew Elvish: "If I am hiring someone new, I look for someone who can talk and present themselves well. You have to be intelligent and articulate. You can be a great designer, but if you can't articulate your vision or make a pitch, you are not really that useful. To be able to discuss your craft is an important part of the business to me."

Tom Kouri: "You have to be able to articulate your ideas verbally. That's part of our culture: we are able to articulate it before we create it."

"Learning to be a more analytical money person was probably the hardest part of building my career as a designer."-Andrew Elvish

MAKING IT

You've worked your way up through the ranks at a design agency and now you have a reputation. Clients ask for you by name. You feel like you've accomplished what you set out to learn about this business, and now, you're feeling a little stifled. You have new ideas that don't quite mesh with the prevailing design philosophies at your agency. With every ad, poster and restaurant menu you see, you think "I could do better."

Maybe it's time to take steps towards a career in freelance design. Maybe it's time to move on to a different type of agency, perhaps one with a world-class clientele or perhaps one that caters to a very specific niche.

It is absolutely time though, to understand that you're now in the business of art.

Here's what our graphic design experts have to say about making the move from interning industry novice to self-sufficient graphic arts professional.

- **STAY UP-TO-DATE WITH THE LATEST TECHNOLOGIES AND TRENDS**
  Rachel Stephan: "Stay current. Graphic design is a very fast paced business and you always need to be learning more about your craft."

- **FOLLOW UP WITH YOUR CLIENTS**
  Tom Kouri: "Good freelancers are curious about the way clients react to their work. You should always, always follow up."

  Denis Dulude: "Once a job is finished and your client has received the completed project, you should always call and make sure they're satisfied. It's smart to say something like 'I've enjoyed working with you and I hope to do it again in the near future.' And then, once in a while, you should remind them of your collaboration by sending a quick e-mail that says 'if you have anything coming up, I'd love to work with you again.'"

- REMEMBER, YOU ARE WORKING FOR YOUR CLIENTS

Tom Kouri: "Although you might have a certain style, it is better to satisfy the needs of your clients or you're not going to make it in this business."

- INVESTIGATE PRICING PRACTICES AMONG YOUR PEERS

Denis Dulude: "I am still not always sure about how much to charge. When I was starting out, I would call people in my field and ask them how much they were charging for similar projects."

Andrew Elvish: "It's important to live by your quotation; you cannot agree to a certain amount and then bill your customer for a totally different amount. This is difficult to do in the beginning. As you grow as a freelancer, you will gain a better understanding of the business aspect of your profession."

- KNOW WHEN TO MOVE ON

Rachel Stephan: "I started as a contract worker, then got a permanent job, and finally became head of a department. That gave me a lot of experience and prepared me for the next step. When I reached the point where I wasn't learning anything new anymore, I decided to take the leap [into self-employment]."

Andrew Elvish: "You have to be flexible about your plans. If it's not working, it's not working. Move on. Sometimes people get caught up in the wrong five-year plan. There's no point in sticking with it. Change it. Turn it into a plan that will work and that will make you happy."

- LEARN FINANCIAL RESPONSIBILITY

Rachel Stephan: "The instability of not having a steady income can be scary. You really have to be able to plan ahead for when times are a little slow."

Tom Kouri: "Save for a rainy day. Know that, as a graphic designer, there will be peaks and valleys. Enjoy the peaks but put aside a little money for the valleys."

FINAL THOUGHTS

Before we send you on your way towards a successful career in the graphic arts, here are a few more nuggets of advice given to us by Denis Dulude, co-founder of 2Rebels foundry.

He reminded us that no matter where you are in your career, no matter how many successful campaigns you have under your belt and packed into your portfolio, satisfying clients is always a challenge. Being at the top of your game doesn't protect you from clients who think they know better than you. Dulude tells us "it is important to learn to say no. Learn that you can't work with everybody." As your career progresses, you will have important decisions to make. Is your artistic integrity or paying your bills more important to you? Can you find a way to balance both? We hope that in your new role as an artistic entrepreneur you come to understand that developing strategies to deal with difficult clients is as important to your bottom line as staying up-to-date with the technical aspects of your trade.

"You need patience," says Dulude. "You need perseverance and patience. Add a little bit of humour and a bit of talent. That's the recipe for success."

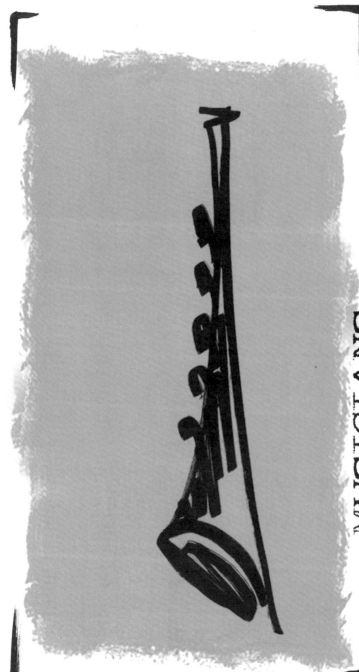

MUSICIANS

"Willpower and desire, when properly combined, make an irresistible pair."
— Napoleon Hill (1937), as quoted by singer Lorraine Klaasen

So you wanna be a MUSICIAN?

The living legends who inhabit the world of music captivate and fascinate fans and critics alike. But down here on Earth, far from the glamour of superstardom, the working musician's life is often fraught with toil and trouble.

We won't lie: making it in music takes more than great pitch and an ear for harmony. But, as you'll read in the pages that follow, if you stay focused, have goals and treat music like the career it is, success is definitely within your grasp. In this section, Montreal-based musicians and a talent developer for the Donald K Donald Entertainment Group share their tips on getting ahead in the music industry.

Musicians work in a wide variety of creative occupations. If our expert advice piques your interest in the business, or perhaps leaves you feeling a little less certain about your future in music, you may want to further investigate the following related fields:

- Accompanist
- Artistic director, orchestra
- Choirmaster
- Concert singer
- Instrumental music teacher
- Motion picture musical director
- Music director
- Music teacher - private, conservatory or studio
- Recording director
- Session musician
- Song writer
- Stage musical director

- Arranger, music
- Choir director
- Choral director
- Conductor, orchestra
- Lyricist
- Music arranger
- Music officer – military
- Musical director
- Record producer
- Rehearsal musician
- Silhouette artist
- Sound engineer
- Street musician

(Source: National Occupation Classification, published by Human Resources Development Canada)

PANEL OF MUSIC PROFESSIONALS

In this section, we interviewed:

SERGE ASSADOURIAN
Artist & Repertoire (A&R) for Donald K. Donald Entertainment Group music labels, including: Aquarius Records, Last Gang Records and Arts & Crafts International. A&R's find and develop talent for music labels.

BLESS
Recording artist, founder of Platinumberg

LORRAINE KLAASEN
Jazz and African music vocalist. She has shared the stage with Patti Labelle, Roberta Flack and Ray Charles, among others

BARBARA LEWIS
Singer, songwriter and editor

TIM RIDEOUT
Composer, producer, independent media specialist

TOM STOWE
Independent songwriter, musician

SCHOOL

As in other performing arts, a solid educational background in music can open doors in teaching or administration should you decide to stop performing at some point. But, our panel of music professionals told us in a near united voice: unless you're interested in working in a highly technical field like sound engineering, hands-on learning in the industry and mentorship under a trusted professional beat formal education hands down.

SOME THINGS JUST CAN'T BE TAUGHT
Bless: "In my field, you can't be taught how to rap in school. It's more about watching great people whose music you respect and studying their work."

IN THE MUSIC INDUSTRY, IT'S ALL ABOUT WHO YOU KNOW
Bless: "It's all about networking in the entertainment business. I think that someone who has hands-on experience is way more valuable to a record company than someone who went to school."

LEARN FROM YOUR EXPERIENCES
Lorraine Klaasen: "It is one thing to take lessons from a teacher and another to go on stage in public, tape yourself, and hear your mistakes. With time, the stage is the best teacher."

Lorraine Klaasen: "My best teacher has always been the public. If they are enjoying the show, then I know I am doing something right. If not, I know I have something to work on."

Musician Barbara Lewis doesn't eschew the idea of school, however, "Getting a degree shows that you were able to finish a project," she said. "The more you know about the technical side of music – theory, arranging, and repertoire – the more control you will be able to keep over your own creations."

But, she cautions, "Don't expect a good music business education in most schools. Not yet anyway." For that, you'll have to rely on educating yourself, including talking to professionals, joining professional organizations and reading books like this one cover to cover.

PORTFOLIO

To land a job in the music industry, a demo of your work is an absolute necessity. The National Occupation Classification survey determined this; our panel of musicians confirmed it.

According to Serge Assadourian, a talent scout with Donald K. Donald Entertainment Group, your demo tape or disk should consist of no more than three songs, and they should be the best you have. "The people listening to your demo will only listen to 20 or 30 seconds of your music. If you don't hook them during that time frame, you won't be getting a call back," he told us. Also, he advises that "a demo doesn't have to be professional studio quality when you're just starting out, but I have to be able to hear it well."

Assadourian also recommends that you have a professionally written resume, including a short biography, along with a list of your previous music experience, your musical talents and other related skills. Musician Tom Stowe adds that you should also include a list of references in your package.

GETTING STARTED

You may lead the choir every Sunday with the spirit of rock in your soul, or maybe you tore the house down at a recent café gig, but don't go diva on us yet. Without practice and professional guidance, you risk pulling the plug on a potentially successful musical career.

The message from our musical mavens is clear: you are responsible for developing your image, your style and your talent and for selling that package to industry pros.

In their own words, here are some tips from our panel on moving your gig from the Metro to Metropolis:

TAKE OPPORTUNITIES THAT ARE RIGHT FOR YOU AND YOUR CAREER

Bless: "I got offered a record deal when I was 13 and didn't take it. I got offered another deal at 16, and didn't take that one either. I only released my record last year. I felt that none of those early offers were giving me the proper promotion and exposure. I wanted to learn the business well enough to make it possible for me to be successful, rather than just throwing a record out there with no knowledge of the business, getting screwed and not getting the kind of promotion I needed."

Barbara Lewis: "Take the time to discover what makes you truly original and remain true to that gift. Don't leap for the wrong success and risk becoming well-known for something that is not you. It is very hard to re-educate your audience about who you are."

HAVE WELL-DEFINED GOALS AND GO FOR THEM

Bless: "I would say that if you believe that you have talent and you are a reasonably intelligent person and other people can see that you have talent, then the most important thing that you need are goals. Then, just go after them."

CREATE OPPORTUNITIES FOR EXPOSURE

Bless: "You need to get out there and create a buzz around yourself. Eventually, opportunities will come knocking if you put yourself in any and all situations where you are meeting the right people and you are getting people talking about you."

Lorraine Klaasen: "I volunteer in the community. I give singing lessons to youngsters and I help out in other ways. That way, people see me and they know me. I develop my audience that way."

WORK FOR FREE

Bless: "When I was starting out, certain people would need filling slots or opening acts. Of course, they would never want to pay me, but I did all these shows for free as a way to get exposure. If you get up there in front of a lot of people often enough, people will start to recognize you. You increase your profile: the more you do it for free, the more you will eventually be able to command."

Serge Assadourian: "Essentially, when you are just getting started, you will want to put on free shows. Eventually, you can bump that up a bit. You can get together with other bands and then you may be able to charge more. Sometimes a bar will pay you to play, other times they will want a cut of your ticket sales. Be vigilant, but at the same time, when you're just getting started, any gig is worth considering."

Tom Stowe: "If the gig would be good exposure for you, then consider doing it for free. Keep in mind that professional musicians will not be pleased (unless they're in the same situation as you). This is a tricky situation, for which I have yet to come across a good solution."

LEARN HOW AND WHEN TO NEGOTIATE FOR YOURSELF

Bless: "You only have a certain amount of negotiating power when you are nobody. Take it or leave it. Don't expect to get what you want on your first deal. But if you become successful, and things go your way, it's your turn to negotiate."

BECOME A COMMODITY

Serge Assadourian: "Record companies will be looking for a track record. If you are meeting with industry types and they decide they like your music, they will ask you 'what have you done in your hometown?' or 'do you have a following there?' These are important things to work on. They'll want to know that you have played a bunch of little shows."

WHEN AN OPPORTUNITY DOES ARISE, MAKE SURE YOU ARE PREPARED

Serge Assadourian: "Sometimes bands will ask me to come and see them play and when I get there, they are clearly unprepared. I won't waste my time with them again."

GET TO KNOW YOUR AUDIENCE AND INVITE THEM TO GET TO KNOW YOU

Lorraine Klaasen: "You have to have a pleasing personality. My personality has played an important role in getting people to come see me. I make each person feel special for coming to see my show."

Tom Stowe: "I may be old fashioned, but building a fan base one person at a time is steady and sure. Playing live allows you to hone your performance skills because you connect with more people each time you get on stage."

LEARN FROM PROFESSIONALS/LEARN FROM YOUR AUDIENCE

Lorraine Klaasen: "Young singers today sing too much like the singers they hear on the radio. They sing in a key that is not theirs. Work with a pianist; they're good at telling you your range. Go and see other performers, go to the theatre. Watch how people there perform."

Tom Stowe: "A musician gets started by playing a lot for their own pleasure, and then playing for other people and listening to what they say. If you listen, they will tell you what they like and don't like. Use that advice to get training in areas in which you have weaknesses. I personally think the best advice comes from members of the audience who know very little about music [technically speaking]."

CONSIDER STARTING OUT WITH AN ESTABLISHED BAND

Tom Stowe: "Of course it's always great to slowly get into performing by playing in a band that's well-known. They do all the work getting the gigs, doing the publicity and organizing the practices. Be aware, however, that you probably won't get a chance to 'shine' on your own in this arrangement. After a while, you'll have to get things going for yourself."

"If you want to be successful, it can't just be about the music. There has to be a balance between your art and your business." – Tim Rideout

MAKING IT

You've done so many charity gigs for free you should be sainted, but taking a vow of poverty is not a necessary part of the musician's lifestyle. There comes a point where you don't want or need to work for free anymore. It's time to take it up a notch, upgrade to better equipment and hire professional musicians to back you up.

To do all that, you need to start earning cash, so it's time to start thinking like a professional and an entrepreneur. You can't do it all, so hire professionals to help you round out the administrative edges of your career. Get educated on things like contract negotiation, copyrights, royalties, marketing strategies and financial tips for stretching your income to last through slow times.

We've also asked our music industry experts for some advice on making your talent work for you.

MAKE A POINT OF MARKETING YOUR BRAND

Bless: "I am willing to make all kinds of concessions, as long as a couple of things are not compromised. One of these is my artistic vision, and another is that my logo, my brand, and my company be on every single thing that I do."

Lorraine Klaasen: "People won't come to see you if they don't know you. Call local radio stations, get interviews. Take initiative."

Tom Stowe: "I think the most effective way to market yourself is to have a lot of people talking about you and saying that you are the hottest upcoming performer around. If you've got a lot of friends and they're willing to cruise chat sites on the Internet repeating your name, that is another way to market yourself.

"Direct communication remains the best: gather e-mail addresses at your gigs and send regular notes on upcoming appearances. The old-fashioned phone and paper letters are also making a comeback. It seems that with all the e-mails being sent around on a daily basis, people are really happy to get a call or a letter, and it sets you apart from the usual mail clogging their inbox."

YOU ARE IN BUSINESS AND THIS IS YOUR JOB: WORK AT IT

Bless: "The music business really is a business. You have to show the right people that you are already making money, or you have the potential and interest to make money."

HIRE PROFESSIONALS TO HELP MANAGE YOUR CAREER

Bless: "There is only so much one person can do. If I am recording, I can't be on the phone keeping things happening. I think that a quality manager for your personal day-to-day stuff is absolutely essential. Also, you eventually need a good booking agent. All of these people are worth the 15 to 20 per cent you paid them, as long as they bring you a certain amount of business."

Serge Assadourian: "Eventually, you need an agent, but not from the outset. Once you have achieved a certain level of success, you will want to hire an agent to get other streams of revenue flowing in.

"When you are negotiating your record contract, it's crucial that you have a lawyer who specializes in the industry to advise you concerning the stipulations of your contract."

LEARN TO NETWORK EFFECTIVELY

Tim Rideout: "Networking is key. Finding contract work is really a matter of who you know. Get out there and always be nice and professional."

Barbara Lewis: "Keeping a good people database is extremely

important when you are committed to being an independent artist. They'll form your audience."

Lorraine Klaasen: "I support in order to be supported. I pay to go to different community events [including events put on by different ethnic groups] and I appear at these events. People see you and then it is easier to invite them to your shows. Basically, I'm not just sitting by the phone, waiting for it to ring. I'm out there and I know what is happening in the community."

STAY INFORMED

Barbara Lewis: "As often as possible, I spend time in bookstores looking at new books in the areas of both business and the art of music. And I read a lot of books on general marketing and promotion as well."

BE RESOURCEFUL AND CREATIVE IN FINDING SOURCES OF INCOME

Lorraine Klaasen: "In June and July, the city thrives. But what happens the rest of the year? That's where the business part comes in. You have to look for other opportunities to continue making money. In my case, I started networking with people, and now I am able to perform in the Caribbean during slower months."

Tom Stowe: "Creativity is the key to breaking out. Play all kinds of venues: coffee shops, art galleries, even hockey games!"

PAY YOURSELF FIRST

Lorraine Klaasen: "At the beginning, my whole idea was to pay everybody first and I'd come home and have nothing. Pay yourself as you go along. There is also a lack of security that [self-employed artists] have, so put something aside for yourself for the future, as you begin to make money."

PRICE IT RIGHT

Tom Stowe: "If you find a club willing to pay you to play, start by suggesting about $100 per band member and watch their reaction, then adjust accordingly. Most reputable clubs will be willing to pay that much for a one-night gig. Outdoor festivals range from zero to $700, depending on their budget, on how much experience you have and what they've heard about you. That's why references are so important."

FINAL THOUGHTS

We asked our panel of musicians whether they considered it important to keep up with trends in popular music. It was here that the true artist emerged and responded in a way that might make the businessperson within cringe.

They conceded that it isn't necessarily musical talent that drives someone to stardom in this industry. Some were quite cynical, saying that big business, driven by image and sex, is behind the gargantuan successes met by only a fraction of artists.

"If you want to be a musician," says Barbara Lewis, "you have to use every ounce of your creativity to find ways to keep doing what you love." The good news, she says, "is that there are still many musicians who are keeping the artistic flame alive."

Like Tom Stowe, for instance: Instead of struggling to keep up with ever-changing fads and follies in the pop music world, Stowe, in short, keeps it real.

"It's better to keep track of who you are and evolve in a way that pleases you," Stowe says. "I don't think it's important to keep current. Just be honest with yourself and try to deliver that honesty in an artistic fashion."

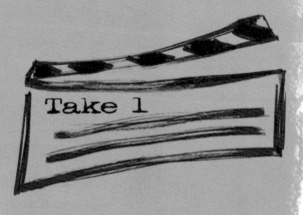

Take 1

FILMMAKERS

"Making your film is only 50 per cent of the work. The other 50 per cent is promoting it, making sure it gets sold." - Paul Shore, Montreal-based filmmaker and Canadian bureau chief, Guerrilla News Network

So you wanna be A FILMMAKER?

The first time you got behind a camera and held it in your hands, you knew there was no place you'd rather be. Your mission is to share your stories by showing your stories. You are a filmmaker.

Whether it's another road trip/buddy film you plan to shoot (this one is different, we know), a 400-minute avant-garde art flick or a take-no-prisoners guerrilla documentary, in artsy Montreal, there will probably be people willing to pay money to see your film.

In this section, we feature the advice of five Montreal-based artists intimately involved in Montreal's film scene. We won't generically apply the term "filmmaker" to them; each does something different in the industry and brings a unique perspective to the discussion.

There are such a variety of occupations in filmmaking that, unless you've done thorough research, spoken to a range of people in the field and are confident that you know which aspect of the industry is right for you, you'd do well to investigate further to see if there is a fit out there that you hadn't previously considered.

Occupations related to film include:

- Film director
- Film writer/Screenwriter
- Film editor
- Film and video camera operator
- Audio and video recording technician
- Film producer
- Director of photography
- Broadcast journalist
- Broadcast technician

(Source: National Occupation Classification, published by Human Resources Development Canada)

PANEL OF FILM AND VIDEO EXPERTS

In this section, we spoke with a variety of people involved in the video and film production scene in Montreal. They are:

AFSANA AMARSY
Co-president of Primesco, one of Canada's largest producers of IMAX films

VITO BALENSANZO
Filmmaker

MAUREEN MAROVITCH
Writer and director at Picture This Productions

PAUL SHORE
Video producer, director, and editor; Canadian bureau chief of GNN (Guerrilla News Network)

EZRA SOIFERMAN
Producer/ director at Perpetuum Productions

SCHOOL

The jury is out on whether an aspiring filmmaker needs a university education to make movies. The short answer is "probably not." But, making great flicks on either film or video requires extensive technical knowledge that goes beyond what you may have picked up shooting old home movies. From counting f-stops to ccds, from 8mm to digital hi-8, if you expect to be taken seriously by your peers, you'd better know how to talk the talk.

A film or communication studies degree introduces you to the technical side of filmmaking. It also allows you to study film history, film styles and the works of the most influential, controversial and important names in film. Film school is also a great opportunity to play with high-tech equipment, and work at a slower pace than frenzied movie sets shooting to deadline.

In the opinions of our assembled experts, a university degree can't hurt and, if you take a proactive approach and follow your teachers' recommendations and advice, can actually prove to be quite helpful. If you decide to enrol in film school, make the most of your experience: network, get involved with as many projects as you can, volunteer and seek out the films and festivals your professors recommend.

Although film school will arm you with an array of skills, our experts concur that when you're looking to make it, no degree beats the experience gained by jumping into the industry wherever you can. "Film is one of the only fields you can succeed in without an education. You go in as an intern or as an assistant, and then you move up in rank," says Vito Balenzano, a Montreal film producer. "It takes years and years to do this, but there is no substitute for experience."

PORTFOLIO

Let's be blunt here: you need a portfolio of your work if you're ever going to be more than the Bringer-of-Lunches or the Giver-of-Coffee on set. A quality portfolio will help you make a lasting impression and might even contribute to your next big break.

- HAVE YOUR MOVIES READY ON DVD AND VHS

Have demos of your work on both DVD and VHS, because different directors will request different formats. Keep several copies on hand at all times so you can distribute demos as needed and submit several applications at once.

- KEEP IT SHORT/GO LONG

You never know if a director will want to see a sampling of your best work, or if they'll want to watch your best production in its entirety. Edit your work down to a smashing highlight reel of your best stuff, but also be ready to present full-length flicks.

- "BUT I'VE NEVER MADE A MOVIE BEFORE. WHAT DO I DO?"

We assume that if you've read this far into the filmmaking section, you have some sort of creative bent. We trust that you're accomplished in whatever medium you've so far chosen to express yourself in.

Don't feel constrained if you've never made a film. Whether you write, take photos, paint or design clothes, show the director that you have vision, talent and boundless creativity by sending a portfolio of the very best of what you do.

"You need two things to make a film: one is a passion, the other is a story."- Paul Shore

GETTING STARTED

You've sat through Andy Warhol's controversial film *Empire*, an eight-hour shot of the Empire State Building, and thought, "I could do better than that!"

Or, perhaps your favourite fruit and vegetable store is closing after serving the neighbourhood for 70 years. Why not immortalize this historic spot, the quirky grocers who ran it and their loyal customers on film?

Or maybe you want to tell a good, old-fashioned love story that unfolds on a winding staircase on St-Urbain Street, plays out on Montreal's most romantic boulevards, and ends in tragedy on the banks of the Lachine Canal.

What now? Although you might have all the talent in the world, if you want to pursue a successful career in film, you still need to pay your dues. Our panel of award-winning filmmakers agreed that the best place to start is at the bottom, and move up from there.

Here is what our experts told us about landing a job in film and making it work for you:

- **CONSIDER VOLUNTEERING ON A SET**

  Maureen Marovitch: "Volunteering is important because although school is great, you don't learn what it's like to work on a set. You'll learn more in a month working in the industry about the professional world than you will throughout your entire degree."

  Vito Balenzano: "When you know which field you want to work in, introduce yourself to the head of that department and tell them you would really like to work in film. Tell them that it's your passion, that you want to learn as much as you can and that you're willing to do it for free, on any project they may have coming up. The 'for free' bit is key. Usually this will get you a call-back."

- **OR, APPLY FOR ENTRY-LEVEL PAYING JOBS: PRODUCTION ASSISTANT, PRODUCER'S ASSISTANT OR RESEARCHER**

  Paul Shore: "In an entry-level position, you want to surround yourself with people who have a lot of experience. Being someone's assistant is a good idea because you learn a lot through osmosis by being on set with them."

- **MAKE SURE YOU STAND OUT FROM THE CROWD**

  Maureen Marovitch: "I get a lot of resumes, especially by e-mail. A lot of them come from students right out of school, so there is not much to distinguish them from one another. If you want me to take notice, you have to find a way to differentiate yourself. Join an association, volunteer, get involved at school; do something that will make your resume stand out."

AVOID FORM LETTER APPLICATIONS

Maureen Marovitch: "I get a lot of letters that I can tell are generic. I get other letters that say, 'I really enjoyed this film you did and that's why I am contacting you.' At least from that I can tell they did their research."

LEARN TO LOVE GRUNT WORK

Vito Balenzano: "Carry the suitcase, carry the camera, get them coffee. Do whatever they ask you to do, do it well, and never complain. It's worth it. You are watching masters of their craft and you are learning a great deal on the job. This kind of experience is priceless."

BE PERSISTENT

Ezra Soiferman: "Whether you are looking for an entry-level position or an internship, approach companies that you would love to work at and apply. You have to be very persistent during the application process. And always make sure you follow-up. You really have to show them you are interested and that you want them to remember you."

GET A DRIVER'S LICENCE IF YOU DON'T ALREADY HAVE ONE. HAVING YOUR OWN CAR DOESN'T HURT EITHER

Vito Balenzano: "A lot of film sets are located in odd places and are shot at odd times of the day when buses aren't running. They won't hire someone who can't make it to the set when they're needed."

CLEAR YOUR CALENDAR AND MAKE YOURSELF AVAILABLE

Vito Balenzano: "The film industry is very fast; it's very spur of the moment. Success has a lot to do with being at the right place at the right time. You might just luck out one day when you're cold calling, and end up speaking with a director who has just fired an assistant or had someone quit on the set. He or she might ask you if you're available to start immediately. When an opportunity arises, grab it."

GET YOUR HANDS DIRTY IN ALL ASPECTS OF PRODUCTION

Ezra Soiferman: "As an intern or an assistant, try to gain experience in all fields, across the board. The insights you will gain, knowing how a film is made from the inside out, will be an invaluable asset to your career."

- JOIN PROFESSIONAL ASSOCIATIONS

Maureen Marovitch: "Associations are great. Many young filmmakers don't join them, but I think that if they did, they would stand out."

"The best thing about associations is that you can meet a lot of successful people and have the chance to volunteer or work on their projects."

"It is as important to be a business person as it is to be an artist." - Ezra Soiferman

MAKING IT

Congratulations. Scorsese came to town and you landed a P.A. job on the set. You befriended an important figure in the Montreal film scene and from then on, the jobs have been coming in steadily.

You've seen the way things work on a set, you've made some key contacts along the way and now you're confident that you have the skills to make and sell really good movies.

But do you really have what it takes to get your film to the big screen? You may have made the movie to end all movies, but unless you have some basic knowledge of the film business, it's more likely to sit in a can than to play in the local multiplex.

We've also asked our film experts for some advice on how to get your film from the editing suite to a theatre near you:

- BE ORIGINAL AND TRUST YOUR OWN CREATIVITY

Afsana Amarsy, co-president of Primesco, one of Canada's leading producers and distributors of IMAX films, advises aspiring filmmakers to focus their energy on being unique. "If you create something truly unique," she says, "everything else, funding your film, marketing it, promoting it, will be that much easier."

- BEFORE YOU MAKE A FILM, THINK ABOUT WHO IS GOING TO BUY IT

Paul Shore: "With TV, usually you pre-sell. You pitch your idea to those in charge of buying projects, and then, when you get the okay, you make your film.

"Sometimes, I invest my time and money and I make part of a film I want to shoot. From this, I get a trailer [a snippet of the film that gives an idea of what is to come] and I use that as my pitching tool."

Maureen Marovitch: "If it's not made for television, that is, if it's a short fiction film, go the festivals route. You really have to do your research for this or you will end up spending huge amounts of money. You want to see at which festivals your film fits."

- APPROACH FUNDING WITH THE SAME CREATIVE ZEAL YOU DO YOUR ART
Ezra Soiferman: "Corporate sponsorship is not easy to get so be entrepreneurial about it. For example, approach a restaurant and ask them for money in exchange for exposure in your movie."

- MAKE A SHORT FILM
Ezra Soiferman: "My best advice for getting your foot in the door is to make a great short film. Team up with friends to complete your project, get it into the festivals. Just get your work out there."

- USE THE RESOURCES THAT ARE OUT THERE
Ezra Soiferman: "Pick up a book about film festival survival, like Chris Gore's *The Ultimate Film Festival Survival Guide*. Read everything you can find about festivals on the Internet. There is so much useful, free information out there."

- DEVELOP A SNAZZY PRESS KIT
Ezra Soiferman: "If you want your work to be out there, try to get publicity from newspapers. Send them copies of your short film along with a well-written press release and photos from the shoot, and then make sure to follow up. Pass your package around to as many people as possible."

-THEM'S SELLING WORDS: WRITE A PITCH THAT WILL LEAVE THEM WANTING MORE
Paul Shore: "Being able to write and deliver an effective pitch is very important. Most producers don't have time to read, so you send them a one-line pitch via e-mail. That line can't just sum up your film; it has to make your film sound original and irresistible. You only have one chance to make that first impression.

"At the end of the day, you need a one-page pitch which you send only once you have been told the buyers want to know more about your project. It has to be tightly written; every word is important and the first sentence really has to hook your reader."

- BE CREATIVE AND DO WHATEVER IT TAKES TO HAVE PEOPLE SEE YOUR FILM
Maureen Marovitch: "If you have a lot of nerve, you can rent a theatre and invite all the people whom you would like to have watch your film. Invite all the big executives. Always doing things the established way won't get you noticed."

Paul Shore: "My films have been shown on a very popular website. The web is not a good way to make money, but it's a great way to advertise and to build a community, an audience."

REMEMBER, YOU ARE WORKING IN A RELATIONSHIP BUSINESS

Maureen Marovitch: "Be nice. If people are volunteering on your project, or even if they are being paid, always remember that they are there. Director is not another way to spell 'dictator'."

"Filmmaking is a team effort. In the long run, people will hire someone who is good and pleasant to work with over someone who is extremely talented but difficult to work with. No matter how talented you are, if you are impossible to work with, at some point all the doors will be closed."

FINAL THOUGHTS

There are ways to get your films seen that won't cost an arm and a leg. For instance, it's relatively inexpensive and easy to create your own online portfolio and personal website. Be sure to tune your web copy for search engines. Include as many words and phrases about you, your background and your special talents on as many pages as possible. That way, when someone goes online to search for "Montreal avant-garde filmmaker," your site will rank high on the list of results.

Most of all, take heart. If ever there was a town to be a young filmmaker in, Montreal is it. From Le Rendez-vous du Cinéma Québécois, Vues d'Afrique and the Jewish Film Festival to the Fringe Fest and International Festival of Films on Art, in this cultural, artistic community, if you make it, they will come.

And take one last piece of advice from award-winning documentary filmmaker, Ezra Soiferman:

"Be your own Picasso. Develop your own unique style. Don't be afraid to get out there and show it, and have endless faith in yourself as an artist."

WRITERS

So you wanna be a WRITER?

Ahhh, the lonely, tormented life of the writer... late nights spent hunched over a rickety typewriter in a dimly lit motel room...coffee stains on every page...demons and muses locked in a bloody battle to be heard through your words.

Well, that's the way your concerned friends and family may have envisioned it for you. Thankfully, this bleak picture needn't be a portal into your future. In fact, the writing scene is alive and thriving in Montreal, and the wordly wise have myriad opportunities to put their talent to work for them.

In this section, we feature the advice of five Montrealers who all write to live and live to write, as well as insights from an editor for the *Montreal Review of Books*. Keep in mind that our panel represents only a small sampling of the many career paths a writer can walk. If our expert advice piques your interest in writing, or perhaps leaves you feeling a little less certain about your future in print, you may want to further investigate the following related occupations:

- Advertising copywriter
- Columnist
- Copywriter
- Essayist
- Interactive media writer
- Medical writer
- Public relations executive
- Scientific writer
- Speech writer
- Book reviewer
- Copy editor
- Editor
- Novelist
- Journalist
- Playwright
- Poet
- Script writer
- Technical writer

(Source: National Occupation Classification, published by Human Resources Development Canada)

PANEL OF WRITERS

In this section, we spoke with:

STEVE GALLUCCIO
Author, playwright. Wrote award-winning play *Mambo Italiano*

STEPHANIE WHITTAKER
Freelance journalist

CHRISTINA MANOLESCU
Poet, author of *The Northern Isle of Dreams*

LEILA PELTOSAARI
Author, self-publisher. Wrote *Illegally Easy Halloween Costumes for Kids, College Cuisine* and *Hey Kids,…Let's Make Gifts*

URSULA JUGEL
Advertising copywriter

MARGARET GOLDIK
Administrator in the cultural field and co-editor of the *Montreal Review of Books*

SCHOOL

The first thing a writer needs is an impeccable grasp of the English language. Hopefully you paid attention in high school the day they taught subject-verb agreement, and while you may not be able to tell us what a dangling modifier is, we hope that doesn't mean you're using them.

However, it takes a lot more than high school English to become a great writer. You should be skilled at composing sound arguments and at conveying meaning in a clear and concise manner. You also need a strong vocabulary and a well-developed critical thinking process.

These abilities may come from reading books, and certainly reading helps keep the mind in top writing form, but there are also important skills that are learned and improved upon by studies at the university level. A university degree, particularly at the graduate level, also allows you to develop expertise and informed opinions about particular areas of interest.

Furthermore, according to the National Occupation Survey* and to any cursory glance at job ads for professional writers, a bachelor's degree or college diploma in fields like journalism, English or communication studies is frequently a requirement.

* Compiled by Human Resources Development Canada.

PORTFOLIO

A writer isn't a writer until someone else says they are. No magazine editor or PR executive or film director is going to hire you to write for them because you say you can. You need a portfolio to show them that you're serious, smart and able to communicate.

If you have never been published, don't worry. While published pieces lend credibility to a writer, editors and publishers know that everyone has to start somewhere...

- NEVER BEEN PUBLISHED? NOT TO WORRY. START YOUR PORTFOLIO BY WRITING ABOUT WHAT YOU KNOW

Write a travel article about a place you've visited, a road trip you've taken or the neighbourhood you live in now. Write a restaurant review, movie review, or product review. Published or not, if it's well-written, editors and publishers will see that you are a talented writer.

Don't be shy to ask people for interviews and include facts or figures gleaned from research as you write these pieces. This is not only a fun exercise, but you may end up with something publishable.

- THE FIRST AND LAST TIME YOU CAN MAKE STUFF UP

If you find yourself applying for jobs that involve a very specific genre of writing and you have no previous experience in this field, fill the gap in your portfolio by creating a stellar piece of writing.

Applying for a job at an ad agency, but have no previous ad writing experience? Find an ad and re-write the copy for it. Or, make up an ad from scratch. Looking to break into PR but have no previous experience? Search online at one of the many sites that post press releases and study how the best are written. Then, write a clever press release about yourself and your job search.

- TAILOR YOUR MATERIAL TO EACH JOB YOU APPLY FOR

Your portfolio of college newspaper articles is probably good enough to land you a junior position as a public relations writer, and your creative writing may get you past the door into an ad agency. However, overwhelming a news editor with poetry samples might not be your best career move.

It's always a good idea to tailor the content of your portfolio to each job you apply for. Before going in for an interview, put yourself in the employer's shoes and think about what kinds of writing samples would most impress him.

PRESENTATION, PRESENTATION, PRESENTATION

Present clean copies of your work. Crumpled newspaper clippings aren't as nice as clean, photocopied or scanned versions.

Present your work in a clean folder or light binder. Consider using page protectors.

Lastly, make extra copies of your work to leave with employers, publishers or editors. Make sure to include a copy of your resume with your contact information.

PUT YOURSELF ONLINE

Consider creating a personal website with versions of your resume and your written work in Adobe PDF format, so the people whom you contact can easily print them out.

This is also an opportunity to show another potential talent: writing for the web.

Be sure to maximize your web copy for search engines. That means you should include as many words and phrases about you, your background and your special talents on as many pages as possible. This way, when someone goes online to search for "Montreal copywriter freelance bilingual," your site will rank high on the list of results.

"You'd think English writers in Montreal were sidelined and poverty stricken. In fact, you can always find someone willing to pay you for your writing." -Stephanie Whittaker, freelance writer

GETTING STARTED

If spending quiet evenings alone with your private diary or word processor is your idea of the writer's life, think hard as you read this section. Many people can't foresee a future without a steady paying job and choose to satisfy their creative urges by writing as a hobby, sharing their creations with family and friends and maybe going so far as participating in public readings every now and again.

But if you're like Steve Galluccio, author of the award-winning play *Mambo Italiano*, and you can't imagine a full-time career that isn't writing, read on for some tips about jump-starting an emotionally and financially rewarding career.

BEFORE YOU THINK 'SELF-EMPLOYMENT' CONSIDER 'EMPLOYMENT'

Stephanie Whittaker: "Young writers should look for a staff job somewhere before going on to freelancing. They need to cut their teeth somewhere before going out on their own."

BE PERSISTENT IN YOUR JOB SEARCH

Stephanie Whittaker (On hounding the editor at the *Montreal Gazette* for a job): "I all but pitched a tent in the newsroom. I waited three hours to speak with the editor. He didn't offer me a job on the spot but I bugged him enough on a daily basis that he finally got tired of me phoning him and hired me."

BEFORE YOU SUMBIT A MANUSCRIPT

Margaret Goldik: "When you are submitting work to a potential publisher, it's important to write an excellent query letter. Do your homework; think ahead to what information you would need if you were a publisher getting tons of manuscripts, and make it easy for them to get the flavour of what you have written."

KEEP LEARNING AS YOU GO

Stephanie Whittaker: "As writers, we tend to be jacks-of-all-trades. We know a little about a lot. As such, we have to read a lot and become self-educated on the things we want to write about. The more you learn, the more you can turn that knowledge into stories."

BE OPEN TO UNEXPECTED OPPORTUNITIES

Steve Galluccio: "Once, I saw an ad in the *Mirror*. It was for a screenwriter looking for a translator for a script he had written in French. I just called this guy up, and he happened to be Emile Gaudreault. He had written *Louis XIX, Le Roi des Ondes*, and was looking to have it translated. Immediately, we started working together; he is the one who opened the door for me on the French side. Emile later went on to direct *Mambo Italiano*."

STUCK FOR A STORY IDEA? THERE'S A STORY RIGHT UNDER YOUR NOSE. FIND IT, THEN WRITE ABOUT IT

Stephanie Whittaker: "Everybody has a story. They may look dull but everyone has a twist, something that's interesting. All it takes is a little scratching at the surface to figure out what it is."

ADOPT A MENTOR

Christina Manolescu: "Find a mentor by going to literary events like book launches, poetry readings, plays. Stick around after a performance and introduce yourself.

"You can also look to your peers and friends. A mentor need not be a genius. The person need not be 'out front' and already widely recognized."

"The money will come if you love what you do and have good business sense."
— Steve Galluccio

MAKING IT

YOUR WRITING IS YOUR BUSINESS. TAKE A PRO-ACTIVE APPROACH TO SELF-PROMOTION AND MARKETING

Leila Peltosaari: "It's like they say, marketing is 99 per cent and writing is one per cent. Sometimes I think that is true. I don't spend money on advertising. I have tried it a few times and it never pans out. Instead, I send 200 review copies to editors of key publications, newspapers or magazines, along with a press release. I target editors [who will see relevance in my book's subject matter.]

"Be creative about your marketing strategy. When I published *Illegally Easy Halloween Costumes for Kids*, I approached UNICEF with a distribution proposition because UNICEF is connected to Halloween. Basically, I try to find offbeat, different ways to market my books. I ask myself 'who would want this book?' and then I pursue these opportunities."

Steve Galluccio: "When I was doing the Fringe Fest, I was the king of self-promotion and that's why I always had the most popular show...

"There was this show I did once, it was a spoof of *The Brady Bunch*... A really good friend of mine was playing Jan. She wore this long blond wig, short shorts and really tight shirt for her costume. When I was looking to publicize my show, I would take her along, in full costume, and we would go looking for an audience.

"I'd bring her to the Main and we'd go into bars and she would do her 'Jan Brady' and invite everyone to watch her perform in the play. I did tons of stuff like that."

CHECK WITH LOCAL BUSINESSES AND ORGANIZATIONS ABOUT SPONSORSHIP OPPORTUNITIES

Steve Galluccio: "When I was doing my stuff independently, I'd look at the play I was doing and if it had gay themes or women's themes, then I'd approach associations actively involved with these groups for sponsorship.

"For instance, when I did *Peter and Paul Get Married*, I went to Divers/Cité and told them I'd donate all of the box office profits for one night to their organization if they could totally fill the theatre. I did this because I knew that through word of mouth the news would spread and people would come see my show.

"I would also approach businesses and restaurants and ask them for money in return for putting their name or logo on my posters. It didn't always work but often it did."

- KNOW YOUR COPYRIGHTS
Stephanie Whittaker: "Protecting your copyrights is a huge issue for freelance writers. It is so easy to pirate information once it appears on the web. You need to keep checking to see if someone has stolen or used your writing. Usually, moral suasion can be used to have the copyrighted material removed, but sometimes legal action has to be threatened as well."

- GET JOB DESCRIPTIONS IN WRITING
Stephanie Whittaker: "You don't necessarily need a written contract and you don't need a lawyer, but make sure you have all the details of what the editor [or publisher, director, etc.] expects from you in writing. That means you should be clear about the exact topic, how you are supposed to treat it, the length and the style of each piece."

- DON'T OVER PRINT
Leila Peltosaari: "If you decide to self-publish, never print 5,000 copies when you are just getting started. One thousand is better, or 500, depending on printing costs. If you start very big, it will be very discouraging not to sell all of them. If you print smaller runs, the cost per book will be more, but it's a safer way to get started."

- KNOW HOW TO PRICE YOUR WORK
Stephanie Whittaker: "Writers.ca has a long table of what writers can charge based on the type of writing they are producing, their years of experience, their background, the number of words and the amount of research and interviewing required to complete the project."

Leila Peltosaari: "When you are self-publishing, it's nice to have pricing that is about eight times your production costs. There has to be room to give a discount; distributors and bookstores will want 50, 60 or even 80 per cent discounts. You have to be able to accommodate these people."

- GET AN EDITOR YOU TRUST
Leila Peltosaari: "Books are immortal. Once you release them, you can't take them back. Have someone go through your work when you are done, someone who is knowledgeable, intelligent and has a good command of the language. You don't want to agonize over stupid mistakes once the book is published."

- WRITE SOMETHING NEW AND ORIGINAL
Leila Peltosaari: "I try to publish books that have very little competition; this has contributed to my success. I always tell other

self-publishers: make something better, make it different or make something that doesn't exist. If you are simply competing with what has already been done, you won't get very far."

- **DEFINE YOUR AUDIENCE AND MARKET TO THEM ACCORDINGLY**
  Leila Peltosaari: "Know who you are writing for and market to them specifically. Editors will not publish you to please you; they'll do it to please their readers. If it is appropriate for their magazine and if it is something that makes their magazine look good, they'll publish it. Don't waste your time with publishers that don't print your type of writing."

- **YOU CAN'T ALWAYS EXPECT TO WRITE ABOUT THE THINGS THAT YOU LOVE**
  Stephanie Whittaker: "Make yourself available to write about topics that aren't necessarily your favourite, unless you don't care about making money. Find out what the market wants and embrace those topics."

FINAL THOUGHTS

It may seem counterintuitive, but our panel of writers is adamant: there are still paying jobs for English-speaking writers in Montreal!

In fact, according to advertising copywriter Ursula Jugel, there is even a shortage of English writers in Montreal, in certain fields like advertising. Moreover, English writers in Montreal who can speak and understand French have an added edge in the marketplace.

One of the burgeoning fields in the city is "localization." Similar to translation, localization is taking French ads and rewriting the copy in English specifically for the Montreal market. This kind of writing allows the writer to be creative in his or her interpretation and can provide a steady stream of work since there are few ad agencies in Montreal that produce English ad copy.

Similarly, according to Stephanie Whittaker, "Toronto publishers don't quite get Quebec, and they are so grateful if they have someone who is bilingual." She also recommends that writers pick up a copy of *Magazine Writing from the Boonies* by Mark Zuehlke for tips on writing from Montreal but selling in the national market.

Lastly, we couldn't think of a better way for this chapter to wane than with Christina Manolescu waxing poetic:

> *"At an early stage in your career, make an office and take your writing seriously in the same way you do your Pilates or balance your cheque book. Strive for excellence; know you'll read to the bottom of everything and just have to start again, so don't go mad. And remember to say thank you to the Creator of the Universe for that."*

PERFORMING ARTISTS

"Hollywood is about commerce, not art. Art can be made anywhere, but if you only want to make art, you'll starve." – Jamie Elman's acting teacher.

So you wanna be a PERFORMING ARTIST?

Montreal is fast becoming synonymous with Hollywood, as big-name productions come to town to take advantage of our (relatively) low-cost talent, first class production studios and stunning urban scenery. But for those in the world of performing arts, "performing" means more than a cameo appearance alongside Hollywood's hottest heroes.

Artists with talent, drive and strong business sense can go on to become celebrities in their own right. And certainly not just on the silver screen. A plethora of performing art icons call Montreal home. In this section, you'll find tips on getting started and making it from professionals representing a broad spectrum of the Montreal performing arts scene.

If, after reading through this section, you're interested in broadening your horizons in the performing arts or if you decide to look at other fields in which you may have transferable skills, consider the related occupations listed below:

- Acting teacher - private or studio
- Art director - motion picture, broadcasting and stage productions
- Artistic director
- Ballet teacher
- Belly dancer
- Broadcasting producer
- Chorus dancer
- Dance instructor
- Director, broadcasting
- Director, radio
- Director, television
- Dramatic reader
- Extra, performing arts
- Narrator
- Performance artist
- Radio director

- Actor
- Art instructor
- Artist
- Ballet dancer
- Ballroom dancing teacher
- Broadcasting director
- Choreographer
- Comedian
- Director
- Director, motion picture
- Director, stage
- Director, video
- Editor, film
- Mime
- Orator
- Producer

(Source: National Occupation Classification, published by Human Resources Development Canada)

PANEL OF PERFORMING ARTISTS

The advice featured in this section comes to you from the following performing artists, all of whom got their start or made their careers in Montreal:

JAMIE ELMAN
Actor. Currently plays "Luke" on NBC's *American Dreams*

LINE GIASSON
Casting Director, Cirque du Soleil

MARGIE GILLIS
Internationally acclaimed solo dance artist and choreographer

DAVID ALLAN KING
Artistic Director, OUT Productions

MARK KRUPA
Actor, writer, photographer

SUGAR SAMMY
Stand-up comic

GARY SAXE
National organizer, ACTRA

JANE WHEELER
Actor

SCHOOL

According to the National Occupation Classification (NOC), many people employed in the performing arts have an undergraduate degree, while one in ten have a graduate degree. The NOC survey also found that, if artists didn't have an undergraduate degree in their chosen field, they probably had a college diploma or other post-secondary specialized training.

Our panel generally felt strongly about the need for professional training, whether done at the university level or in private classes. For instance, Line Giasson, casting director at Cirque du Soleil said that "for many disciplines, we expect our performers to have studied their art extensively."

Other thoughts on school were:

-SCHOOL GIVES EMERGING PERFORMANCE ARTISTS CREDIBILITY
Actor Mark Krupa says having a diploma can come in handy when searching for a part.

"There are many parts for young actors, and agents and casting directors know that they might not find actors in that age range with a ton of experience," says Krupa. "Because of that, they will consider someone who doesn't have experience but has an education in drama or acting."

AN ADVANCED DEGREE IS A SECURITY NET FOR THE FUTURE

As a performance artist just getting started, you probably haven't thought about what you'd do if you could no longer perform. As remote as we'd like that possibility to be, it is important to have a contingency plan.

Teaching young talent the craft after you acquire some experience for example, is a fulfilling way to pay the bills. David Allan King, Artistic Director at OUT Productions, suggests that a graduate degree is useful, if not absolutely necessary for a career in teaching.

STUDYING ENLIGHTENS THE MIND AND BRIGHTENS THE PROSPECTS

A great vocabulary is a strong asset for any actor, especially for those involved in improv work or stand-up comedy. Comic Sugar Sammy says going to school not only broadened his vocabulary but also his networks of contacts.

EVERYBODY CAN USE A LITTLE EXTRA HELP

"It's very important to get a decent amount of training, especially if you haven't done theatre school," says actress Jane Wheeler, "even if you think you're a natural." She suggests checking out some part-time beginner programs offered by studios specializing in improvisation and on-camera work.

IT ALL DEPENDS ON WHAT KIND OF PERFORMER YOU ARE

Performers specializing in extreme sports, for example, aren't expected to have extensive training because there just isn't any available, said the Cirque du Soleil's Line Giasson. But for a gymnast, she said, the Cirque requires extensive training because there is the expectation of a certain degree of technical ability.

On the other hand, says actor Jamie Elman (whose application to Concordia University's theatre program was turned down), many actors come out of theatre school thinking "now I've graduated, so now I'm an actor." Theatre schools, he says, make you a polished, classically trained thespian, but they don't necessarily prepare you for work in front of a movie camera.

Be aware that some theatre schools don't permit students to take on professional acting jobs during their studies, although they usually provide financial assistance to compensate for the lost income. Many young actors think this is unfair, but David Allan King sees it another way. "Take it if you can," he says. "There's nothing more beneficial than being able to focus full-time on your own artistic development."

PORTFOLIO

Our panel of performing artists was loud and clear: you need a head shot in your portfolio and you need it done right! The head shot, usually in 8 x 10 format, will be sent along with the rest of your background material to casting directors and, eventually, to your agents.

Not all professional photographers can produce a decent head shot so ask peers or union representation to recommend someone who can do a great job. Actor Jamie Elman recommends visiting with several photographers until you find one with whom you feel comfortable.

Professional head shots can be expensive but the performing artists who spoke to us were unanimous. This is a necessary investment early in your career that will have big payoffs later. Elman says, "If you can only afford one thing at the beginning of your career, spend it on head shots."

So, should you run off to the salon for a drastic haircut and have the seasonal color palette painted on your face before your photo session or is au naturel the way to go? According to Jamie Elman, your head shot "shouldn't be a glamour shot. It should look like you, but better." He also stressed the importance of seeing your eyes clearly in the photograph.

What else needs to go into your portfolio? You need a proper resume. List all the work you've done, broken by medium (theatre, television, film, radio, etc.). For an emerging performer, the information listed on your resume also goes beyond school and past experience to include eye and hair colour, special skills (like tightrope walking, for instance), languages spoken and accents that you're capable of performing.

You should also include a demo reel. In addition to your headshots, having this produced professionally in a studio is another worthwhile investment.

- If you are interested in doing voice work for commercials, cartoons or voice-overs, have a voice demo produced. Actress Jane Wheeler recommends that you record yourself reading magazine ads aloud in different accents and tones of voice to demonstrate your range.
- If you already have numerous clips from TV and film work, hire a video editor to produce a montage of your clips.

- If you're looking to be an acrobat, gymnast, circus performer or other physical performer, send in a video of your performances along with your resume. If you don't have any professional performances to show, have someone film you at work in a gym or studio.

David Allan King also recommends that performing artists put their portfolios online on a professionally designed website. Along with photos and resume, King suggests including video demo clips on your website.

"Don't swallow someone else's 'no.' Chew on it, taste it, then spit it out. You have to be prepared for rejection and you have to persevere beyond it."- Mark Krupa, actor.

GETTING STARTED

You were the sweetheart of your high school production of Swan Lake or your passion for performance led you to a myriad of long line-ups where you and scores of wannabe stars waited for hours until a casting assistant answered your prayers and made you an extra on the latest, biggest production to hit the town.

But now you're ready to make the move forward with your career. You've got the talent; you just need a little direction. Read on for our expert directions on getting started on the road to success.

- START AT THE BOTTOM AND WORK YOUR WAY UP FROM THERE

Margie Gillis: "Enjoy working from the ground up. As you develop through the basics, you learn important business skills."

Sugar Sammy: "Do open mics for a few months until you get better and better. Sign up for workshops offered at comedy clubs. Also, watch a lot of stand up. Rent stand up [on video]. The more you are exposed to it, the more you absorb it."

Jamie Elman: "The more you know about every aspect of the business, the better. I took a job as a production assistant while I was shooting *My Hometown* to fill in the three days a week that I wasn't shooting. I had to make coffee in the morning and clean out ashtrays at night, but I got to see exactly how a TV crew works."

- ON THE OTHER HAND...

Mark Krupa: "I don't recommend doing a lot of extra work. It's great once or twice to get a feel for the way things evolve on a set but beyond that, you get typecast as an extra."

BE HONEST, BE YOURSELF

Jane Wheeler: "A lot of actors think they should embellish the 'special skills' section of their resume. It's far better to be honest and say, no I don't have those skills, but I'd love to come in to the studio and learn from someone who does.

"One time, very early on in my career, I foolishly responded to a call put out by the CBC knowing I didn't quite meet their requirements. My resume said I had dancing skills because I had done some ballet and jazz dance in school, but the CBC was looking for someone specifically with ballroom dance experience. The audition ended with me looking very foolish in front of some very important people."

Line Giasson: "When auditioning, be yourself. This is very important. Our casting team wants to hire unique, talented individuals. Don't try to imitate someone else; be who you are. If you're talented, the casting agents will see it."

LEARN FINANCIAL RESPONSIBILITY

Jamie Elman: "Get educated on things like how much commission an agent should receive and be responsible about keeping track of your expenses."

BE WELL-PREPARED FOR AUDITIONS

Mark Krupa: "Less is usually more when it comes to auditioning. When you're starting out, focus on your craft at auditions. Directors and casting agents see so many people. Being overly friendly or chummy with them will usually turn them off. Also, when you are going to an audition, you always have to be prepared to improvise. Directors are looking for artists that are malleable. They want to know that they can shape you into your character."

David Allan King: "Dress professionally, aim for a relaxed body and voice, and remember, directors and casting agents often hate being looked at directly or used as a point of focus."

IF YOU STAGE IT, THEY WILL COME: LEARN TO MARKET YOURSELF

Jamie Elman: "Get colleagues and friends together for small plays, or stage scenes together. Invite agents, casting directors and other industry professionals that you'd like to meet and that you think should see your work."

David Allan King: "How to get your foot in the door is one of the biggest and toughest questions to answer. One of the ways that has proven successful for many young performance artists that I've seen is to ride it out a little longer with the less visible productions—the ones we all must do, often with little or no revenue-and invite as many people to see the production as possible."

Sugar Sammy: "If the comedy clubs aren't helping you out, organize your own shows. When I was just getting started, I would do everything I was offered: bars, night clubs, charity events and school events. And while you're there, invite other comics in to watch you perform."

FIND AND LEARN FROM A MENTOR

David Allan King: "No one ever tells you where the good mentors to train with are! Eventually, you find out what kind of artist you are and what kind of methodology works for you. Once you know these things, study other performer's work. This should give you a good idea about the kind of performing artist with whom you want to train.

"When you do find a mentor, ask them for a letter of support, pick their brains whenever possible and have them refer you if you need a reference. Most importantly, watch their work and analyze it. Decide what it is about what they do that attracts you to them."

Sugar Sammy: "Often, established comics in the audience will come up to you after your performance and comment on your work. Learn to take advantage of them and their expertise."

REJECTION HURTS, BUT LEARN TO USE IT AS A STEPPING STONE

David Allan King: "Too often, people just scold themselves with that sour inner voice. If you are constructive enough and can find out what you can do better the next time, you can really turn things around."

Sugar Sammy: "Everyone bombs once or twice. The first time I bombed, I quit for two years. That was a bad decision. You have to keep going. Tape yourself at every show and watch it to see what worked and what didn't. Learn from your mistakes and just make sure you don't make them again."

Margie Gillis: "Even if you are rejected once, it doesn't mean that you won't audition for a new director in a year who will want to hire you. You can't hear 'no' and just sit on your haunches and say 'okay.' You have to contact those people, find out what went wrong and do it again."

JOIN A PROFESSIONAL ASSOCIATION AND A UNION

Unions and associations protect performing artists' rights. These organizations also offer encouragement and assist in your development. Some offer workshops with potentially influential artists and mentors.

Gary Saxe: "Joining a union will both protect you and make information about your rights readily available."

SHARE WITH AND LEARN FROM YOUR PEERS
Sugar Sammy: "Get together with other performers and form writing groups to run your stuff by each other."

Gary Saxe: "When you are looking for parts, for an agent, or other information about the industry, a good place to start is to speak to colleagues."

KNOW WHERE YOUR PERSONAL STRENGTHS ARE AND WHERE THEY CAN LEAD YOUR CAREER
Jane Wheeler: "Whether you are too fat or too skinny, whether you have brown hair or blonde hair, that's who you are. You need to be confident in yourself and you need to feel that you are strong in at least one particular area."

ACT PROFESSIONALLY
Jane Wheeler: "Keep calling the casting director to remind them about you. But, you do have to get a sense of when you might be harassing people. Those are important cues to pick up on for the audition process."

THERE IS NO "I"…
Line Giasson: "There aren't any stars in our shows; the star is the show. The circus involves a great deal of teamwork so we need to see people who are willing to work with a team and are able to contribute to that team. As an emerging artist, leave your ego at the door."

"You have to understand that you are a commodity. You are in the business of selling yourself."
-Jamie Elman, actor

MAKING IT

You've landed a gig with the performing arts troupe of your dreams. In your dreams, mind you, it was you demanding the 63 bottles of imported mineral water and heaping bowls of M&M's (minus the red ones, of course) for your dressing room. It wasn't supposed to be you picking out the red M&M's for some other diva.

Still, you get in front of the casting director on a few occasions and you impress him with your classical interpretations or wild impersonations. You've been a character in search of an author for years and finally you've found someone willing to write you into a starring role.

Our panellists warn us that it's not all glitz and glam at the top, though it is a lot of fun once you get there. Professional performing artists in Montreal have to work hard at promoting themselves and their artistry.

While Montreal is known as a culture-friendly city, it's still not always easy to keep believing in your power and purpose as an artist.

Read on for what our panel of experts had to say about making it as a performing artist.

- FORM A SUPPORT NETWORK

David Allan King: "One of my biggest mistakes was not taking the time to connect socially with other artists. You have to plan to include some social down time to connect with others and, well, schmooze."

- PLAN FOR YOUR FINANCIAL FUTURE

David Allan King: "Another big mistake was not investing my money properly. You have to live pretty frugally as an actor to get by and afford the expenses that the career demands."

Jane Wheeler: "There are hot times and slow times. No one expects to be working all the time, but when it's good, it's good. You just have to remember to put some money aside for those leaner times."

- USE TRANSFERABLE SKILLS TO STAY BUSY—AND GET PAID—DURING SLOWER TIMES

Jane Wheeler: "When things are a little slower or there aren't any big productions in the city, I supplement my income with voice work for radio ads."

Jamie Elman: "When you're an unemployed actor, it's easy to wallow in self-despair and self-pity. I used my degree in English to get a job as an ESL (English as a second language) teacher. It's a life outside of acting, but it still gave me the chance to perform in front of an audience."

- YOUR BODY IS YOUR GREATEST ASSET: TREAT IT WELL

David Allan King: "You really have to take care of your body and voice. Your body is an instrument that needs constant fine tuning."

- STAY AHEAD OF THE SCENE: KEEP TRACK OF PRODUCTIONS COMING TO MONTREAL

Jane Wheeler: "Find out what productions are coming to town and get a hold of the scripts early on. For instance, when the Centaur announces their season, I get a hold of the plays and find out what kinds of parts there might be for me."

- MARKETING 101: YOU ARE THE BRAND – SELL YOURSELF

Sugar Sammy: "You have to be a good self-promoter. You've got to get out there and market yourself. Treat your career like a business."

Jamie Elman: "You are the president and CEO of You, inc. You also have agents and publicists who work for you and to whom you pay commission and who are important cogs in the business. You have to run your career like a good business person would."

IF YOU DON'T ALREADY HAVE A WEBSITE, GET ONE

Sugar Sammy: "I have a personal website, with information about me, my act and details about where and when I will be performing. At the end of every show I do, I hand out my card with my website address on it. When people visit the site, they're asked to sign up for a mailing list. That way, I have a collection of addresses and I can send out updates and personalized invitations for my shows."

KNOW WHEN TO HIRE AN AGENT

Sugar Sammy: "Don't get an agent until you feel like you can't handle your career yourself. When I look for an agent, I'm looking for someone who can open doors that I can't. I'm not interested in people whose contacts are the same as mine."

Jane Wheeler: "Having an agent when you start to land more roles makes things easier. They'll do a lot of the legwork (like meeting with casting agencies) that you'd otherwise have to do."

Gary Saxe: "Your agent is a partner in your career. Always remember, an agent works for you and not the other way around. When you are interviewing agents, look for one who sees your career in the same light you do. For example, you may want to do a lot of voice work; your agent may not see you this way. You have to get an agent that shares your vision and that will be honest with you."

KNOW YOUR RIGHTS

Gary Saxe: "You can always contact unions, even if you are a non-member. If you are working on a union contract, and you want more information, contact your union. If you are looking to hire an agent, again, you can call a union and they will give you general feedback."

GET EDUCATED ON PRICING STANDARDS

Gary Saxe: "Industry standards are negotiated for you, when you are doing a union role. You cannot work for less than that. You can try to negotiate for more, but they can't pay you less."

SURROUND YOURSELF WITH ADEQUATE SUPPORT

Margie Gillis: "There is a dilemma for artists: you want to spend your time doing art and you have to eat. If you're spending your time creating budgets or writing for grants, you're focusing on the business aspect and then you aren't practicing your art. Insofar as it is possible, surround yourself with people that support your vision and help you with the administrative end."

BE AN AMBASSADOR FOR YOUR ART

Margie Gillis: "It is extremely important that we lobby those people in a position of power for arts funding. Look to the government; ask your politicians to support the arts. If they can't provide funds, ask them to speak about the value of artistry in the community.

"Always try to leave a place better than when you came. Clean the dressing room before you leave. Tell the theatre how much you appreciated them. Remember, you are not just representing yourself, you're representing your art form."

FINAL THOUGHTS

If there was one message that emerged from the interviews with our performing artists, it was, in the words of David Allan King, "Make yourself noticed."

According to King, making it as a performing artist requires risk-taking and going with your gut instinct. After all, he says, "you only have one life that you know about." Don't blow your chances by not taking yourself and your career seriously.

Talk to professionals who are in a position to help you: union representatives, accountants with small-business clients, agents whom you trust, publicists and colleagues whom you admire. Investing early on in your artistry will mean a lifetime of returns and rewards.

FINE ARTISTS

There is a constant need for art." – James Simon, painter

So you wanna be a FINE ARTIST?

Remember how much fun you had the first time you experimented with a finger painting kit? Remember how you clutched those Crayolas in your stubby little fingers and drew all over the brown paper laid down on the kitchen table?

If you still enjoy the thrill of creating your own worlds on blank canvas, then this chapter is for you.

In this section, we offer help and advice from five Montrealers making headlines as painters and illustrators.

Finding a steady source of income as a fine artist isn't always easy. You may want to consider supplementing your career as a fine artist with other work. As a highly creative individual, you likely have transferable skills that can be put to use in the following related occupations:

- Creative Designers and Craftspersons
- Creative and Performing Artists
- Photographers, Graphics Arts Technicians and Technical and Co-ordinating Occupations in Motion Pictures, Broadcasting and the Performing Arts

(Source: National Occupation Classification, published by Human Resources Development Canada)

PANEL OF FINE ARTISTS

The advice featured in this chapter comes from the following artists:

SUZANNE DURANCEAU
Illustrator

JOSE HOLDER
Comic book artist, Illustrator

JOSÉE NADEAU
Painter

SUSAN PEPLER
Painter

JAMES SIMON
Painter

SCHOOL

While they agreed that there were some benefits to studying fine arts in a professional program, the artists interviewed for this section felt that true talent and vision is developed outside of an academic environment.

According to our experts, time spent studying your art in school gives you the opportunity to:

- **LEARN TRANSFERABLE SKILLS**
  Illustrator Suzanne Duranceau says having a diploma means worrying a little less about income during slower periods. "Your diploma might help you get a job as a graphic artist or a teacher when money is a little tight," she says.

- **NETWORK WITH PEERS AND PROFESSIONALS**
  Duranceau also says that a school environment provides students with a great sense of community and a wonderful opportunity for networking.

While painter James Simon sees some benefits in studying painting in a university or professional program, he says fine arts programs don't teach students enough about life.

"I think you have to know something about living," he says. "You have to be some sort of philosopher. You have to have a spiritual side and a clear, unique view of the world to be a true artist, and the last place you're going to find this is in a university."

Internationally renowned painter Josée Nadeau thinks that life experience, along with learning from artists whom you admire and trust, provides the best education a painter can get. "School teaches discipline, but you can be self-taught and be a great artist," she says. "I think mentors are very important and not just one but several from various disciplines."

PORTFOLIO

In our interviews, we were told that your success in fine arts depends entirely on your reputation, and your reputation begins with your portfolio.

- STREAMLINE THE WORK SHOWN IN YOUR PORTFOLIO

James Simon suggests that the collection of images in a portfolio should have a theme. If your work is too scattered and varied, you risk confusing the viewer. "I have seen a lot of portfolios in my life, and they tend to be really mixed up," he told us. "You come away as a viewer not really knowing what a person can do, or thinking that they just dabbled in a few things and never did anything well. Make two or three portfolios if you have two or three areas of expertise. But keep your portfolio very simple and consistent," he says.

Duranceau adds that the images included should all be of the same style and quality. "If each piece is executed with a totally different style, people won't remember you. You have to personalize your work; you need a signature style."

Painter Josée Nadeau urges artists to show an evolution in the pieces they present. "Your body of work has to tell a story," she says.

- KEEP YOUR PACKAGING SIMPLE

Simon warns fine artists not to use packaging that is "too wild or flaky. You don't want the packaging to overwhelm the art," he says.

- KNOW WHAT FORMAT POTENTIAL CLIENTS WANT

"Each client may want to see something a little different, or want the material presented in a specific way," says Simon. "Galleries for example, might require a certain criteria or format. This isn't the time for rebellion. Give them what they ask for."

Painter Susan Pepler stresses the importance of labelling each slide or image that you present in your portfolio. "You should always include the title of each piece, as well as its dimensions and the medium used to create it."

- MAKE IT PRESENTABLE

Even though you may be showing samples from several years ago, Susan Pepler says it is important that the protective pages in your

---

portfolio should always look "new and crisp." Replace them as soon as they start to look worn, she says. "It can be expensive, but it's worth it."

PUT YOUR PORTFOLIO ONLINE

Jose Holder considers this a crucial aspect of your self-marketing campaign. "You need someplace where people can visit your body of work," he says. "They need to be able to download samples for themselves and find contact information."

"Whether you are an artist or an entrepreneur, you have to be ready to seize opportunities." –
James Simon

GETTING STARTED

If you are reading this, you are closer to reaching your goal than you think. You probably have more artistic talent than 95 per cent of people on the planet. You have a lot of paintings or illustrations under your belt. You're probably one of those people who watched every episode of *The Joy of Painting* on PBS with the late Bob Ross. (Heck, you probably remember the name of his pet squirrel!)

But how do you let the world know that you are out there? What do you need to do to make the shift from part-time painter or illustrator to genuine artist?

Our experts say that you need to start with a vision. Ask yourself where you want to be in one year. Write your goals down and, in a year, pull out the list to see if you have achieved your objectives, and readjust your career plans accordingly.

Here is what else our experts had to say about starting out in the arts:

CONNECT WITH SUCCESSFUL ARTISTS

Susan Pepler: "Seek advice from successful artists rather than relying on less successful ones."

DEVELOP CLEARLY DEFINED GOALS

Susan Pepler: "If you don't have a mission statement or a vision of what you want and where you want to go, get one. Find your path. You may have to revise it along the way, but at least you will avoid getting sidetracked."

KNOW HOW TO MARKET YOURSELF AND YOUR ART

Josée Nadeau: "Learn that a 'no' doesn't always mean 'no.' Look for ways to get around it. You could gain experience in sales, and then apply those skills to selling your art."

Suzanne Duranceau: "You need to produce promotional material that you can leave with potential employers when you show them your portfolio."

Josée Nadeau: "Get the media interested; it's really important to constantly promote your art."

- LEARN TO NETWORK AND SOCIALIZE

Jose Holder: "Making friends and contacts in the field will get you further through word of mouth than hitting the pavement. Because artistic communities are so small, jobs are passed along from friend to friend, from contact to contact. You develop this nice camaraderie. Furthermore, meeting with people who work in your field will give you a better sense of rates, of job expectations, of the demands of working in different fields, and what you will be expected to know on the job."

James Simon: "Artists with more social skills tend to do better. Social skills are really important [when it comes to selling your work]. Artists tend to be afraid of interaction, partly because they are different and partly because they have less of a base to start from. It is from that socializing that the most promising relationships [for selling your work] will emerge."

Jose Holder: "Conventions are a great place for illustrators to network. It's nice to be able to sit down and rub elbows with older, more experienced artists and have some of their life experience and their skills rub off on you."

Suzanne Duranceau: "Join an association and befriend other artists."

- NETWORKING IS A KEY TOOL FOR EMERGING ARTISTS

Suzanne Duranceau: "School is where people begin to form their networks and when they graduate, they will remember their friends and their classmates. You should also join an association related to your work and befriend other artists there, and attend events like vernissages as well."

- REMEMBER THOSE THAT HELPED YOU ON YOUR WAY UP

Suzanne Duranceau: "When someone gives you a break or a hand, don't forget this. Try to return the favour whenever possible. It's a small industry, so it pays to be nice."

MAKING IT

You think your paintings are better than most stuff you see in galleries. Younger painters are now coming to you for advice. Things are looking great. You are on the right track. But how can you continue to grow as an artist? What is the next step? How can you use your talents and experience to generate more income?

We've asked our panel of experts to share their thoughts about making it as a fine artist in Montreal:

HAVE A LIFE OUTSIDE OF YOUR ART

James Simon: "Volunteering is always a great way to meet people who are outside your social milieu. If all your friends are artists, you are not going to sell your work. There is no economy in that."

THINK GLOBALLY

Susan Pepler: "Don't limit yourself to galleries in Montreal. Apply to galleries outside of the city. When you travel, always check out the local galleries and find out what their requirements for submission are."

James Simon: "Canada is a tough place because people don't spend as easily. In the USA, people are easier to sell to. I also think that Americans are more respectful of artists and of the entrepreneurial spirit. I always tell local artists to make inroads into the United States if they can."

FIND A GALLERY WHERE THE STYLE MESHES WITH YOUR OWN

Susan Pepler: "Visit galleries and apply to those where your work fits and where it will be hanging next to work that you respect. At the same time, you have to be realistic. You have to show your work somewhere to become known, so you may not get to exhibit in your ideal gallery right away."

LEARN HOW TO PRICE YOUR WORK

James Simon: "Art is obviously worth the time and materials that you put into it. It also has a uniqueness that makes it worth something. The power of its intellectual statement adds to its worth and it's worth something because it is pleasing to the eye. When it comes to setting a price however, it's what you think you can get away with.

"If you sell on your own, you won't get the same price the galleries will get because, as far as the public is concerned, galleries give paintings social acceptance. You can't do that on your own without a huge amount of effort. So, you are always going to be a bit under priced, but you aren't paying any commission.

"My belief is to price modestly and make sure you have enough to get by. Don't try to become rich on one painting. The more you sell, the more people will see your work and potentially want a piece of your art. If the price is modest, more people are going to see your work and more people are going to be able to afford your paintings."

SPECIAL CONSIDERATIONS IF YOU ARE COMMISSIONED TO CREATE A PIECE

James Simon: "I try to encourage people to give me their ideas at the beginning of the project before the painting is actually started, while there is still time to adjust. I find some way for them to write this down so that they retain some responsibility for what they say."

MAKE THE MOST OF DOWNTIME

Jose Holder: "Work on your portfolio, network, and incorporate new aspects into your art. Explore your creativity and re-evaluate your approach. Experiment with different styles. Basically, it's a good time to shake things up a bit."

START THINKING LIKE AN ENTREPRENEUR – INVEST IN YOUR CAREER

James Simon: "You need to be able to manage your money. You need to figure out how to create a structure for your business, how to save tax.

"I don't believe that people should be working under the table; they are just condemning themselves to being a kind of second-class citizen. It's not really the way to go. Do business in an open and transparent way, and learn how to do that well. There are real financial benefits to working that way."

Suzanne Duranceau: "Invest in a computer. This will prove to be invaluable to your business. Your computer will allow you to communicate with local and international clients, it will allow you to send sketches for approval quickly and cheaply, and the Internet will allow you to research images."

Jose Holder: "You have to be prepared, which means that you have to invest time and money in your tools, in your supplies. This covers everything from rulers, to markers and mechanical pencils. These things are fairly expensive, but many of these elements will last, so you only have to buy them once. If you are really serious about your career, this is an essential investment."

ᐧ KNOW YOUR LEGAL RIGHTS
Suzanne Duranceau: "It's important to retain rights to your images. Sometimes employers won't offer this as an option. I often choose not to do these jobs. I realize that I may lose customers this way, but when I retire or if I lose my artistic ability, all I have is my body of work so this is important to me."

FINAL THOUGHTS

As James Simon says, "there is a constant need for art because people need nice things for different reasons." Translation: the market for fine arts is always open.

Montreal has many art collectors who are your potential customers. But, as you learned in this section, don't limit yourself to one place. The United States is a great market for art and you should explore all the avenues open to you. Lots of people want to buy your art. They see exceptional beauty in the same things that you do. But they need to be reminded about your art, which is where your marketing and business skills will come in.

Remember that this business is built on reputation, and, as Suzanne Duranceau says: "You are only as good as your last job. Performing well is really the only job security."

So, practice your craft. Get out there and meet new people. Join associations. Volunteer. Set short-term goals and check to see that you've reached them. Build your reputation one person at a time. And, most importantly, have fun.

FASHION DESIGNERS

So you wanna be A FASHION DESIGNER?

When most people think of fashion design, the fashion world's most stylish names are conjured up: Calvin Klein, Donna Karan, Vera Wang, all waltzing down an Italian catwalk in front of an audience filled with the world's most beautiful people.

But, let's face it, creative design isn't the exclusive domain of New York, Paris and Milan. Walk into many chic Montreal boutiques and you'll find the racks are filled with gorgeous creations from homegrown designers. Of course, if you're reading this because you have a passion for fashion, you're already well-acquainted with Montreal's fashion scene. In fact, you could probably name ten hot local designers before you even make it to the checkout counter.

In this section, we feature stories and advice from four well-known Montreal fashion designers, and the director of jewellery design at the upscale national jewellery retailer, Birks.

Graduates of design programs engage in a wide variety of creative occupations. If our expert advice piques your interest in design, or perhaps leaves you feeling a little less certain about your future in fashion, you may want to further investigate the following related fields:

- Clothing designer
- Couturier
- Fashion designer
- Fur designer
- Window display designer
- Costume designer
- Fabric designer
- Jewellery designer
- Shoe designer
- Patternmaker

(Source: National Occupation Classification, published by Human Resources Development Canada)

PANEL OF FASHION DESIGNERS

In this section, we spoke with a variety of authorities on the fashion business in Montreal. They are:

MARNIE BLANSHAY
> Owner, Lola & Emily

MARION CAMERON
> Director of design, Henry Birks & Sons Inc.

SARA ELDOR
> Fashion designer and teacher at The International Academy of Design and Technology

EVE GRAVEL
> Fashion designer

HILARY RADLEY
> Principal designer at Hilary Radley (women's wear) and Radley (men's wear)

NADYA TOTO
> Fashion designer

SCHOOL

According to the National Occupational Classification (NOC), an aspiring designer usually needs a university degree or college diploma in design to land their first internship or job in the industry. Our panel of experts concur. They tell us that you pick up necessary technical skills in school that you'd be hard-pressed to learn on your own.

Design school allows a student to:

- **STUDY TEXTILES**
> "Many young designers think they can just flip through magazines all day and be a designer," says Hilary Radley. But to be a great designer, she says, it takes an intimate knowledge of textiles, including familiarity with fabric, colour, texture and draping, best gained through an appropriate course of study.

- **ACQUIRE TECHNICAL KNOW-HOW**
> Sara Eldor believes school is essential to the success of young designers: "School teaches you the basics. You can have all the talent in the world, but if you haven't mastered the technical side of your craft, your talent will not be enough."

- **HONE DRAWING SKILLS**
> Radley also stresses the importance of drawing well, another skill

that should be honed in design school: "For me, drawing is fundamental. I sketch all the time. Drawing is how you get your ideas down on paper."

PORTFOLIO

To land a job in the industry, a portfolio of one's work is essential. This is not only the results of NOC research, but what our Montreal fashion experts tell us as well.

- **INCLUDE HAND-DRAWN SKETCHES ALONG WITH COMPUTER-RENDERED ONES**

    Radley and Toto both stress that a young designer's portfolio should always include hand-drawn sketches.

    "I can read a lot from hand-rendered work," says Toto, "and as I flip through a portfolio, I can tell a lot about the candidate's personality."

- **INCLUDE EVERYTHING FROM ROUGH SKETCHES TO PHOTOS OF FINISHED DESIGNS FOR YOUR MOST ELABORATE PROJECTS**

    For some of your more elaborate designs, Marion Cameron, the Director of Jewellery Design at Birks, recommends including your initial conceptualization, the research that went into the design, pictures and sketches showing the progression of the project, as well as photos of the completed design. "By showing what led to the projects you are presenting in your portfolio, you are also showing that you can take something from a very rough idea and carry it through to the finished product."

- **CONSIDER INCLUDING A FEW PIECES OF OTHER ARTWORK IN YOUR PORTFOLIO**

    Cameron suggests including a small sampling of other artistic work in your portfolio, if you have some.

    "It's always good to see other things an artist can do because I might decide I like this artist for a position he or she hadn't considered," she says.

GETTING STARTED

You may think that you've read enough *Vogue* and *Glamour* magazines to know what the fashionistas of St. Denis Street and Madison Avenue want to wear. You may feel divinely driven to dress the masses in your glam-inspired collection of couture Creations-with-a-capital-C. Our experts, however, think otherwise.

Successful Montreal-based designers are unanimous: an internship or an entry-level position are the standard means of getting started in the industry and a sure-fire way to meet the people and make the connections you'll need to get ahead.

Here is what our experts told us about landing an internship and making it work:

- **SUBMITTING YOUR PORTFOLIO IS ONLY STEP ONE. IT'S WHAT YOU DO AFTER THIS THAT COUNTS**

    Hilary Radley: "Landing an internship is really a matter of getting your portfolio to the companies for which you want to work and then hammering away on the door until you get an answer. I get a lot of resumes and I don't even know where half of them end up. I know that sounds terrible, but the point is that it's really about being pushy."

    Marion Cameron: "You have to be prepared to walk the streets and knock on the doors of places you think you'd like to work, and then make sure you talk to somebody there."

- **LOOK FOR A GOOD FIT: YOUR SENSE OF STYLE SHOULD JIBE WITH THAT OF YOUR EMPLOYER**

    Hilary Radley: "Wanting to learn and being willing to work isn't enough to get a job with a designer. For me, their tastes have to level with mine. Ideally, when we look at designs or when we flip through magazines, we like the same things."

- **TAKE ANY JOB IN THE INDUSTRY: IT'LL HELP YOU GET YOUR FOOT IN THE DOOR**

    Marion Cameron: "Two very successful jewellery designers I know started in the industry by pulling wax in the factory. They wanted to be designers, but they started by doing manual labour."

    Ève Gravel, a hip Montreal designer, suggests that emerging designers take any position in fashion as opposed to another paying job. "That way, you get the experience you need and it keeps your manual skills in practice."

OFFER TO WORK FOR FREE
Because nothing can substitute for experience, you might want to consider volunteering. Many designers do not have the financial resources to hire a paid intern. However, if you offer your services for free, they might be willing to take you on as an intern.

RESEARCH FUNDING OPTIONS
Consider applying for a wage subsidy. Consult your local employment center for details concerning funding options. Finding alternative means of funding your internship will work as an effective incentive for someone to hire you, as a portion of your salary will be covered for a specific period of time.

LEARN TO LOVE GRUNT WORK
Nadya Toto: "An internship means getting involved with all aspects of production, from packing boxes to cutting threads to ironing. It's not a waste of time; this is when you get to see how the industry works from the inside out."

SHOW THAT YOU ARE WILLING TO WORK AND EAGER TO LEARN
Nadya Toto: "I'm most impressed with interns who are interested in learning and willing to do whatever they are asked to do without complaining. […] No designer is going to bring in an intern and say 'dream up a collection.' That comes later. What young designers need to remember is that they have to work their way up, step by step."

MAKE YOURSELF VISIBLE TO THE PEOPLE THAT COUNT
Sara Eldor: "One way of doing this is to go to work dressed in a dynamic way. Wear something that you actually designed. A patternmaker might see you and say 'Oh! I love what you're wearing!' and that's your opportunity to tell them you made it. Everything is presentation; self-presentation is just as important as product presentation, or portfolio presentation. Remember, you're selling yourself. You're letting them know what you're good at, and down the line, they'll remember you when they need someone with your skills."

STICK WITH IT: THE PAY-OFF IS WORTH IT
Sara Eldor: "I always tell my students that before they start their own thing, they need at least three to five years experience in the industry. This gives them a chance to really get familiar with all aspects of the business."

KEEP A WELL-MAINTAINED CATALOGUE OF YOUR WORK
Sara Eldor: "Take photos of everything you do. Even if you don't think it's that important, take a picture and keep it."

"You cannot give up. You can never give up. The people who made it are the ones who didn't give up. There are a lot of talented people out there who just couldn't hack it."-Hilary Radley

MAKING IT

So, you landed that all important first job in the fashion industry. You probably learned more about the business in your three to five years on the inside than you could have in a lifetime of design school. You saw a side of the industry your teachers never told you about, and you've lived to tell the tale.

But now, your head is crammed with thousands of ideas on how to dress the world, your creative juices are throbbing through every vein in your body. You eat, drink and dream design. It's time to put your creativity to work for someone else: you.

Relax. You knew this day would come. Now is the time to concentrate on business financing, accounting and marketing which, you'll soon learn, are every bit as important to your success as the cut and colours of your spring collection.

We've also asked our fashion experts for some advice on getting your creations from the cutting floor to the catwalk and beyond.

- **INVEST IN A BUSINESS BASICS COURSE**
  Being self-employed isn't easy. As you get started, you will realize that being a self-employed designer involves much more than just sketching and sewing. Learning about business basics in a structured environment will save you both time and money, as it will help you manage the business side of your craft. Hilary Radley agrees: "In design school, they didn't teach any business basics, which is a mistake. I learned the hard way…"

- **START BY SELLING ON CONSIGNMENT***
  Sara Eldor: "In many cases, stores aren't going to buy from someone without experience. But when they hear 'consignment,' the door usually opens for you. The vendor has nothing to lose and a potential money-making designer to gain."
  *Consignment: This means you leave your products with select vendors for a specified period of time. They will sell the items on your behalf, usually keeping a percentage of the sales. At the end of the period, the vendor returns the unsold items to you.

- **DON'T OVERPRICE/ DON'T UNDERPRICE**
  Nadya Toto: "Do your research. Visit stores that sell items similar to your own and take note of the prices on the merchandise. Today, brand names are still important, but if a young designer comes out with something really special and unique, name or no name, people will buy it."

Sara Eldor: "Don't be greedy in the beginning when you are pricing your work. This will backfire very quickly."

Marnie Blanshay: "It's not the buyer's job to price a designer's items. Designers have to know how much they have to charge for their pieces."

KNOW THE STORES YOU APPROACH AND ASK YOURSELF 'WILL THEY REALLY SELL MY PRODUCT?'

Ève Gravel: "Start by researching the style of each boutique and find stores that your clothes would be well-suited to. Then, decide which store would be your number one choice, number two and so on, and approach them in this order."

Marnie Blanshay: "The finishing on the clothing is really important. Especially if small designers are using home sewing machines. It shouldn't look home made if that's not the look of the store."

AND…WHEN YOU'VE FOUND A STORE WILLING TO SELL YOUR WORK, RESPECT THEIR SALES TERRITORY

Ève Gravel: "Your best bet is with independent boutiques that thrive on being unique. If a store on St. Denis picks up your collection, don't try to sell it to another store a few blocks up."

LEAVE A LASTING (AND POSITIVE!) IMPRESSION

Marnie Blanshay: "Small designers don't realize how much stuff buyers see. You need to leave some kind of calling card to jog the buyer's memory. Have something concrete to give as a teaser to get your foot in the door like professionally taken photos of your work, a well-designed postcard, or even a sample."

"Also, call in advance or show up at appropriate times. Don't come in on Saturday morning when I won't have time to deal with you."

DRESS FOR SUCCESS

Sara Eldor: "If you're going to work in design, you have to look good. To me, it's a no-brainer. If I am meeting with a buyer, I concentrate on really putting myself together. Again, it's about selling yourself. You'd be surprised at how many people don't realize this."

Marnie Blanshay: "If you're trying to target a sophisticated clientele, you need to be sophisticated yourself."

KNOW YOUR OWN STRENGTHS: HIRE OTHERS TO DO THE REST

Hilary Radley: "One of the strengths I've had is the ability to know I can't do everything well. Manufacturing was not one of my fortes and administrative work isn't high on my list either. So I concentrated on what I was good at: designing, conceptualizing, starting with a fabric and getting to the final product. I hired others to take care of the parts that, for me, were weaknesses."

FINAL THOUGHTS

Our panel of experts had some other great tips. For instance, many experienced and successful designers still count on the help of mentors. You may consider approaching a designer whom you admire to be your mentor as you develop your own business.

Both emerging and successful designers gain a great deal from joining industry associations or forming their own casual groups of likeminded entrepreneurs. This opens the door to great networking opportunities and provides a much needed support system to the newly self-employed designer, stepping out for the first time.

Be patient and perseverant. Without these attributes, all our experts agree, you are most definitely in the wrong business.

Oh, and one more thing. In the words of Nadya Toto:

"Have a goal, be ambitious, stay motivated and be self-sufficient. You have to have guts. If someone tells you 'no, you're not good enough,' take it as a challenge to prove them wrong."

PHOTOGRAPHERS

"There is not one clear path to success in photography." – Sara Cameron

So you wanna be A PHOTOGRAPHER?

You've been fascinated by still images your whole life. It continually astounds you how a story can be told through a series of frames. Perhaps photography began as a hobby and then blossomed into a way of life.

Now, you plan to embark on a journey, camera in hand, to capture the struggle for democracy in some far-off land. Or perhaps you want to photograph beautiful landscapes closer to home. We're sure you have the skills behind the lens to get your project off the ground, but do you have what it takes to get your work out of the darkroom and into the spotlight?

In this chapter, we offer help and advice from four Montrealers who all started small, but today are all well-known in the photography field.

Photographers are employable in a number of fields. If you're unsure where your talents would be best put to use consider the related occupations listed below:

- Aerial photographer
- Evidence photographer
- Forensic photographer
- Medical photographer
- Photographic technician
- Photojournalist
- Police photographer
- Scientific photographer
- Street photographer

- Commercial photographer
- Finish photographer
- Industrial photographer
- News photographer
- Military photography technician
- Photomicrographer
- Portrait photographer
- Racetrack finish photographer

(Source: National Occupation Classification, published by Human Resources Development Canada)

PANEL OF PHOTOGRAPHERS

The advice featured in this chapter comes from the following experts:

SARA CAMERON
Photographer

PENNY COUSINEAU-LEVINE
Chair of the Department of Visual Arts at the University of Ottawa, author of *Faking Death: Canadian Art Photography and the Canadian Imagination*

SOLANA RYAN
Photographer

LINDA RUTENBERG
Photographer

SCHOOL

Our panel told us that, while school isn't a strict requirement, it still provides a stepping stone into the world of professional photography.

"In 1920, if you decided to be an artist, people would have told you to move to Paris or New York," says Penny Cousineau-Levine. "There, you would have found communities of artists just like you." But times have changed, she says. "Today, if you don't want to do an undergraduate degree, talent might take you there, but it will probably take you much longer."

According to our experts, studying photography in school gives you the opportunity to:

- **LEARN FROM EXPERTS WHO WANT TO HELP YOU**
  "Studying with professionals means you get constructive feedback from those that are in a position to help", says Cousineau-Levine.

- **LEARN AT YOUR OWN PACE**
  "When you're working, you don't have as much time to explore your craft," says Linda Rutenberg. "Going to school really gives you the time to research and explore your art."

- **NETWORK WITH PEERS AND PROFESSIONALS**
  Both Cousineau-Levine and Rutenberg agree that an academic environment provides students with a great sense of community. "It also permits you to learn about other photographers' ideas and it's a great source of inspiration," says Rutenberg.

SCHOOL WILL GIVE YOUR ART A CONTEXT IN WHICH TO GROW

Penny Cousineau-Levine: "Pursuing a Bachelor of Arts accelerates the development of your art because you aren't re-inventing the wheel, and you aren't reiterating what has already been done. Talent always exists in a context; a plant has to be in earth to grow."

DISCOVER THE TOOLS THAT BEST SUIT YOUR NEEDS

Other than photographic artistry, Solana Ryan says a course in photography will teach you practical things, like how to choose the best hardware and equipment to do what you set out to do.

Solana Ryan sums up the school debate best when she says: "Fine art photography and commercial photography don't see eye to eye in school, but a good photographer needs both."

PORTFOLIO

Our photo experts tell us that, to get started in the industry, a C.V. and a portfolio of your work is a must.

"EIGHT TO TEN EIGHT BY TENS"

When photographer Solana Ryan submits a portfolio, it includes a sampling of about eight to ten pieces of her best work, printed on 8 x 10 paper. She says it's best to include both colour and black and white prints. Penny Cousineau-Levine suggested that you can also submit slides of your work or a CD-ROM with photos in digital format.

Always inquire ahead about the type of portfolio you will need to submit and conform to the stated guidelines.

SHOW A PROFESSIONAL PRODUCT

Linda Rutenberg says the contents of your portfolio should be "well directed and well edited," and that the printing should be of impeccable quality. "Everything should be printed on the same types of paper," she says, "and there should be a sequence to them which reflects the thought that went into preparing the portfolio."

Whenever you meet a potential client, Solana Ryan recommends leaving something memorable behind, such as a unique and creatively designed business card,

HAVE AN ARTIST STATEMENT AND A PROJECT PROPOSAL ON-HAND

If you are looking to put together a show or an exhibition, you should prepare an artist statement and a project proposal to present along with your portfolio.

Penny Cousineau-Levine: "Your artist statement is a one-page description of what your project is about. Along with this, you should prepare a project proposal which details what you would like to do. It should describe the size of each image, how many images will be included in the project, the materials you intend to use, etc."

- INCLUDE A SLIDE/ IMAGE LIST

Penny Cousineau-Levine: "Always include a slide list, or if you are using CD-ROM, a list of the images featured on it. Include information about materials, dates and dimensions."

"Many young photographers have this notion that the art world is waiting for them. It's not."
—Linda Rutenberg

GETTING STARTED

Your friends took you to see a Mapplethorpe exhibit and you didn't bat an eye. You've participated in a number of photo shoots and thought, "yeah, but wait till they get a load of me." You may be ready to burst into the world of art photography, but is the world of photography ready for you?

Don't quit your day job just yet. Our experts told us it takes time to develop a name in the industry and cultivate a loyal clientele. That will come with talent, vision and a lot of hours spent honing your craft.

Here, in their own words, is what our experts told us about getting started in photography:

- THE ROAD FROM PHOTOGRAPHY LEADS OFF IN ALL DIRECTIONS

Sara Cameron: "We're everywhere! It depends on what you want to do. There is medical photography, portraiture, photojournalism, fashion photography, advertising photography, fine art. You can work for the government or the armed forces. You can be independent."

- BE PATIENT AS YOUR CAREER GETS OFF THE GROUND

Solana Ryan: "It takes about three to five years to develop a good clientele."

Linda Rutenberg: "You have to start at the bottom, just as everyone else did, and work your way up. You have to get to know people, build relationships, show your work and ask for feedback. It takes time and unrealistic expectations aren't going to get you anywhere."

- USE REJECTION CONSTRUCTIVELY
Penny Cousineau-Levine: "Have the courage to ask for feedback. When you go back to pick up your portfolio, acknowledge the rejection, but ask how you might improve for next time."

- LEARN TO MARKET YOURSELF
Sara Cameron: "Make your work and abilities known. Be honest with yourself: are you making a genuine effort to meet people and find work?"

Linda Rutenberg says that emerging photographers need a website, business cards and the ability to articulate their ideas and their vision to market themselves well.

Penny Cousineau-Levine: "It is very important for young photographers to get involved with artist-run centres. Volunteer, make contacts, and get involved in anyway you can. As you meet new people, they will become familiar with your work, and later down the road, if they are putting together an exhibition, they might think of you. You really have to get out there as much as you can."

- BE TECHNOLOGICALLY PROFICIENT AND ADAPTABLE
Linda Rutenberg: "You have to be able to work digitally as well as being versed in the old processes and techniques."

- CONSIDER A JOB AS A PHOTOGRAPHY ASSISTANT
Sara Cameron: "Some people assist for years before they get started on their own. A lot of good photographers are professional assistants. They make a really good living and they are invaluable on a shoot."

- TAKE ADVANTAGE OF EVERY OPPORTUNITY THAT COMES ALONG
Sara Cameron: "Never turn down something new without a really good reason. You never know where it could lead."

"Hard work will be remembered and rewarded, but not always in the way you'd expect."– Sara Cameron

MAKING IT

Great, you landed a gig as a photography assistant to the city's premier wedding photographer. You learned as much about portraiture and proper lighting in those years as you did about bookkeeping, networking and managing raging brides. You've got a pretty good sense of what it takes to be self-employed in the arts.

Now, you're ready for your journey. You have the technical know-how to pull it off, combined with confidence in your creative vision and a strong belief in the value of your work.

We've asked our panel of experts to share their thoughts on making it as a professional photographer in Montreal:

GET YOUR WORK EXHIBITED

Penny Cousineau-Levine: "More than getting your work published, exhibiting is how you put yourself on the map. This is how you establish yourself as a professional artist.

"Montreal artists are very lucky because there is an extensive network of artist-run centres [galleries]. You can submit your work to them and they'll consider it for exhibition."

Linda Rutenberg: "I think you have to deserve an exhibition. Exhibitions should be a thoughtful evolution of work that has been developed over an extended period of time. The longer you stick with a project or theme, the more developed your work becomes."

AVOID EXHIBITING IN BARS, BISTROS OR CLUBS

Penny Cousineau-Levine: "This isn't a great way to get out there. It might even bring you down. You won't gain a professional audience at a bar."

HAVE A LIFE OUTSIDE OF PHOTOGRAPHY

Sara Cameron: "Have something that gets you away from all the stress and chaos at least once a day. The photographers I know who have something outside of photography to distract themselves are by far more content and successful than those who live and breathe photography alone."

LOOK FOR SPONSORSHIP OPPORTUNITIES

Penny Cousineau-Levine: "It's surprising where you can get sponsorship from. Bottom line: don't be afraid to ask. Big businesses will sponsor events, like openings, because it's a tax write-off and, to a certain extent, it gives them credence."

⁻ FIND A GALLERY WHOSE STYLE MESHES WITH YOUR OWN
Linda Rutenberg: "When you are looking for a gallery, you should seek out those which are suitable for your artwork. It's very difficult to find a good match, but you have to find a space where your work fits in."

⁻ GET EDUCATED ON PRICING STRATEGIES
Linda Rutenberg: "Don't give away your work for nothing. In the end, under pricing will come back to haunt you, and will devalue the quality of your work and that of others. Consult with peers on their pricing and hourly rates before you offer a quote."

Solana Ryan: "It depends on your years in the industry, but for starters, charging $70 to $80 an hour is about right."

⁻ CONTINUE YOUR SELF-MARKETING CAMPAIGN
Solana Ryan: "You need a mailing list so that you can keep your clients updated on your work.

FINAL THOUGHTS

The best news of all is that Montreal is a great city for up-and-coming photographers. We have a well-established support structure for emerging artists, including the network of artist-run centres mentioned by Penny Cousineau-Levine, and a population that prides itself on a reputation for culture and high art.

It is very important to stay abreast of the cultural scene in Montreal and abroad, as well. Read trade publications, attend exhibits, surf the Internet, travel. As Cousineau-Levine cautions, "you have to understand where your work is situated within the contemporary context. Art is a discourse, and to enter this discourse, you have to be aware of what is going on around you."

And take one last piece of advice from Linda Rutenberg:

"Making it as a photographer is not always easy. You are working for yourself, so you have to be able to sell yourself and you have to be self-motivated. There is a lot of good work out there. You have to be resourceful, you need to have business skills and you have to really believe in your dream."

RESOURCES

Below you will find a list of resources that can help you establish and fund your business, promote your work and defend your interests. This section is divided into three subsections: **Organizations and Associations, Granting Agencies and Festivals.**

Please note: We have endeavoured to make our resource information as accurate, complete and up-to-date as possible. Nevertheless, this is not a complete listing of every organization serving Quebec artists, and the information listed below is subject to change.

ORGANIZATIONS AND ASSOCIATIONS

ALLIANCE OF CANADIAN CINEMA, TELEVISION AND RADIO ARTISTS (ACTRA)

1450 City Councillors, Suite 530, Montreal, QC H3A 2E6
Tel.: (514) 844-3318
www.actramontreal.ca and www.actra.ca
montreal@actra.ca

ACTRA is a national union representing more than 20,000 Canadian performers working in English. It strives to increase work opportunities for its members and it negotiates, safeguards and promotes its members' professional rights.

Eligibility:
A performer must be cast in six roles on an ACTRA contract (three for visible minorities or disabled performers) in order to be granted full membership.

Fees:
Yes. Please consult the website for more information.

ARTEXTE INFORMATION CENTRE

460 St. Catherine St. West, Suite 508, Montreal, QC H3B 1A7
Tel.: (514) 874-0049
www.artexte.ca
info@artexte.ca
The Artexte Information Centre offers reference and research support for students, artists, curators and other arts professionals.

ASSOCIATION DES COMPAGNIES DE THÉÂTRE (ACT)

C.P. 1321 Succ. Desjardins, Montreal, QC H5B 1C4
Tel.: (866) 348-8960
jobinja@videotron.ca

The ACT represents non-profit French-language theatre producers in

Canada. It offers guidance to its members and organizes training sessions. Services are offered exclusively in French.

Eligibility:
Services are offered only to non-profit organizations.

Fees:
Yes. Please consult the website for more information.

ASSOCIATION OF CANADIAN PUBLISHERS (ACP)

161 Eglinton Avenue East, Suite 702, Toronto, ON M4P 1J5
Tel.: (416) 487-6116
www.publishers.ca
admin@canbook.org

The ACP represents more than 140 Canadian-owned book publishers. Its aim is to encourage and promote the writing, publishing and distribution of Canadian books.

Eligibility:
Open to book publishers.

Fees:
Varies based on the project.

ASSOCIATION DES PRODUCTEURS DE FILMS ET DE TÉLÉVISION DU QUÉBEC (APFTQ)

1450 City Councillors, Suite 1030, Montreal, QC H3A 2E6
Tel.: (514) 397-8600
www.apftq.qc.ca
info@apftq.qc.ca

The APFTQ represents the vast majority of independent film and television production companies in Quebec. It offers its members consulting services, negotiates collective agreements with artists' associations and technicians' unions, and intervenes on matters such as co-production, copyrights and cultural diversity.

Eligibility:
Grants are available only to students of the Institut national de l'image et du son.

Fees:
$150 annual fee per enterprise, plus a percentage of production budgets; $250 fee for associate members.

ASSOCIATION DES PROFESSIONNELS EN AUDIO

1097 St. Alexandre St., Suite 302, Montreal, QC H2Z 1P8
Tel.: (514) 878-9875
www.aspraudio.org
info@aspraudio.org

The Association des Professionnels en Audio promotes the quality of audio through continuing education courses and by representing the interests of its members to official organizations and cultural associations.

Eligibility:
Must agree to respect professional ethics.

Fees:
Yes. Please consult the website.

ASSOCIATION OF ENGLISH LANGUAGE PUBLISHERS OF QUEBEC/ASSOCIATION DES ÉDITEURS DE LANGUE ANGLAISE DU QUÉBEC (AELAQ)

1200 Atwater, Suite 3, Montreal, QC H3Z 1X4
Tel.: (514) 932-5633
www.aelaq.org
aelaq@bellnet.ca

The AELAQ encourages and promotes the publication and distribution of books published in English in Quebec. It offers professional development seminars, co-operative marketing initiatives and a forum for sharing information. It also publishes the Montreal Review of Books.

Eligibility:
Open to publishers or those interested in publishing.

Fees:
Ranges from $50 to $100 a year, based on annual sales.

BLUE METROPOLIS FOUNDATION

661 Rose-de-Lima, Montreal, QC H4C 2L7
Tel.: (514) 932-1112
www.blue-met-bleu.com
info@blue-met-bleu.com

The Blue Metropolis Foundation organizes numerous activities throughout the year in order to bring together writers and readers from different worlds and linguistic backgrounds. It hosts an annual literary festival and offers a variety of educational programs, including writing workshops, a lecture series, a writing contest and an Internet distance-learning program.

CANADIAN ACTORS' EQUITY ASSOCIATION (CAEA)

44 Victoria St., 12th Floor, Toronto, ON M5C 3C4
Tel.: (416) 867-9165
www.caea.com
info@caea.com

The CAEA is a professional association of performers, directors, choreographers, fight directors, and stage managers working in live performance theatre, opera and dance in English Canada. It seeks to improve the working conditions and opportunities of its members by negotiating and administering collective agreements and by providing information, support and benefit plans.

Eligibility:
Must have a signed Equity contract.

CANADIANACTOR ONLINE INC.

www.canadianactor.com
contact@canadianactor.com

CanadianActor Online is a national, online education and information resource for actors. With discussion boards moderated by industry professionals, it's a great place to discuss and learn about the acting business.

Eligibility:
Open to all.

Fees:
$25 for a one-year subscription.

CANADIAN ARTISTS AND PRODUCERS PROFESSIONAL RELATIONS TRIBUNAL (CAPPRT)

www.capprt-tcrpap.gc.ca
info@capprt-tcrpap.gc.ca

CAPPRT is a federal government agency which certifies artists' associations as eligible to represent self-employed artists in bargaining for scale agreements with broadcasters and federal government institutions, and to deal with complaints of unfair labour practices and other matters brought forward by artists, artists' associations and producers pursuant to the Status of the Artist Act.

CANADIAN ASSOCIATION FOR PHOTOGRAPHIC ART (CAPA)

31858 Hopedale Ave., Abbotsford, BC V2T 2G7
Tel.: (604) 855-4848
www.capa-acap.ca
capa@shawcable.com

CAPA is a non-profit national organization for professional and amateur photographers, camera clubs and others with an interest in photography. It publishes a quarterly magazine, Canadian Camera Magazine, hosts the annual Canadian Camera Conference, and supports exhibitions and competitions throughout the year.

Eligibility:
Open to all.

Fees:
$25 for students, $45 for other individuals, and $60 for families (two people at the same address).

CANADIAN BROADCASTING CORPORATION (CBC)

1400 René Lévesque Blvd., East, Montreal, QC H2L 2M2
Tel.: (514) 597-6000
www.cbc.ca/montreal
englishcommunications@cbc.ca

As Canada's national public broadcaster, the CBC provides radio and television programming in English and French that informs, enlightens and entertains. This programming is distinctively Canadian, actively contributes to the flow and exchange of cultural expression, contributes to a shared national consciousness and identity, and reflects Canada's regions as well as its multicultural and multiracial nature. The CBC offers internships.

CANADIAN FILM AND TELEVISION PRODUCTION ASSOCIATION (CFTPA) MENTORSHIP PROGRAM

605-151 Slater St., Ottawa, ON K1P 5H3
Tel.: (613) 233-1444 ext. 224 or 1-800-656-7440
www.cftpa.ca
nmp@cftpa.ca

The CFTPA Mentorship Program supports on-the-job training that allows individuals to obtain hands-on work experience in film and television production. It serves as a complement to formal education and enables participants to make important industry contacts.

Eligibility:
Open to members of the CFTPA.

Fees:
Membership fees vary by region.

CANADIAN INDEPENDENT RECORD PRODUCTION ASSOCIATION (CIRPA)

30 St. Patrick St., 2nd Floor, Toronto, ON M5T 3A3
Tel.: (416) 485-3152
www.cirpa.ca
cirpa@cirpa.ca

CIRPA is the national trade association representing the English-language, Canadian-owned sector of the music industry. Its activities are designed to maintain a strong and economically stable independent music and sound recording industry in Canada.

Eligibility:
Open to all who are involved professionally with the music industry, either as musicians or producers, or through related fields.

Fees:
Range from $399 to $1,500 depending on the type of membership.

CANADIAN INTELLECTUAL PROPERTY OFFICE (CIPO)

Place du Portage I, 50 Victoria St., Gatineau, QC K1A 0C9
Tel.: (819) 997-1936
Hearing impaired only TTY: (819) 997-2848
www.cipo.ic.gc.ca
cipo.contact@ic.gc.ca

CIPO is the federal government agency mandated to accelerate Canada's economic development by encouraging invention, innovation and creativity. It administers the intellectual property systems in Canada (patents, trademarks, copyrights, etc.,) and promotes Canada's intellectual property interests worldwide.

Fees:
There are fees for applying for patents, trademarks and copyrights. Consult the website for more information.

CANADIAN RECORDING INDUSTRY ASSOCIATION (CRIA)

1200 – 890 Yonge St., Toronto, ON M4W 3P4
Tel.: (416) 967-7272
www.cria.ca
info@cria.ca

CRIA is a non-profit trade organization that represents the interests of Canadian companies that create, manufacture and market sound recordings. CRIA supports Canadian recording artists through a broad range of services in the areas of representation and advocacy; marketing and communications; copyright reform and anti-piracy; and statistical analysis.

Fees:
Yes, based on class of membership. Consult the website for more
information.

COOP ST-LAURENT DES ARTS

4633 St. Laurent Blvd., Montreal, QC H2T 1R2
Tel.: (514) 289-1009
www.coopstlaurent.org
service@coopstlaurent.org

Coop St-Laurent des Arts is dedicated to creating and maintaining an
urban space devoted to artistic development in Montreal. It operates an
art supply store and low-rent art studios, and offers art classes.

Fees:
Membership is $25 a year, $15 for students.

CULTURAL HUMAN RESOURCES COUNCIL/CONSEIL DES RESSOURCES HUMAINES DU SECTEUR CULTUREL

201- 17 York St., Ottawa, ON K1N 9J6
Tel.: (866) 562 1535
www.culturalhrc.ca
info@culturalhrc.ca

The Cultural Human Resources Council works to strengthen the
Canadian cultural workforce by providing leadership and innovative
solutions to human resource issues and to better the HR environment
within the cultural sector. It offers a broad range of activities, including
job recruitment, networking, internship support and career and
professional development tools.

Fees:
Some fees apply for career and professional development tools.

DOCUMENTARY ORGANISATION OF CANADA/DOCUMENTARISTES DU CANADA (DOC)

126-215 Spadina Ave., Toronto, ON M5T 2C7
Tel.: (416) 599-3844 or 1-877-467-4485
www.docorg.ca
info@docorg.ca
Quebec Chapter: cifcquebec@sympatico.ca

DOC is a non-profit organization representing the interests of
independent film and video makers in Canada. It hosts regular
membership meetings and workshops, publishes the magazine Point of
View, and hosts events during the annual Hot Docs Canadian
International Documentary Film Festival.

Eligibility:
Full or Associate Membership for individuals involved in the documentary filmmaking industry. Others can join as a Friend of the DOC.

Fees:
Vary by region, but generally in the $100-a-year range.

FEDERATION OF CANADIAN ARTISTS

1241 Cartwright St., Granville Island, Vancouver, BC V6H 4B7
Tel.: (604) 681-8534/681-2744
www.artists.ca
fcaoffice@artists.ca

The Federation of Canadian Artists promotes art, artists, and art education through courses and gallery space.

Eligibility:
All membership applications are reviewed by jury.

Fees:
Yes. Consult the website for more information.

FÉDÉRATION QUÉBÉCOISE DU THÉÂTRE AMATEUR

C.P. 977-181 Bois Francs Blvd. South, Victoriaville, QC G6P 8Y1
Tel.: (819) 752-2501
www.artscite.com/fqta
fqtafita@bellnet.ca

The Fédération Québécoise du Théâtre Amateur promotes amateur theatre in Quebec through a series of contests and workshops. It advertises productions on its website free of charge, administers an insurance plan and rents wardrobes.

Fees:
$30 for individuals, $60 for groups, and $120 for corporations.

QUEBEC MUSICIANS' GUILD/GUILDE DES MUSICIENS DU QUÉBEC

2021 Union, Suite 800, Montreal, QC H3A 2S9
Tel.: (514) 842-2866
www.guildedesmusiciens.com
guildedesmusiciens@hotmail.com

The Quebec Musicians' Guild promotes and represents the interests of freelance musicians. It offers its members a broad range of services, including contract management, legal assistance, financial counselling and travel assistance. Its written contract sets basic minimum fees and working conditions for musicians.

Eligibility:
Open to professional musicians.

Fees:
Yes. Consult the website for more information.

INDEPENDENT MEDIA ARTS ALLIANCE (IMAA)

4550 Garnier, Montreal, QC H2J 3S7
Tel.: (514) 522-8240
www.imaa.ca
info@imaa.ca

The IMAA is a national arts service organization that advances the interests of the media arts community in Canada. It publishes a monthly newsletter, organizes an annual conference on media arts and advocates on behalf of the media arts.

Fees:
$100-$300 per year, based on membership classification.

THE LEAGUE OF CANADIAN POETS

920 Yonge St., Suite 608, Toronto, ON M4W 3C7
Tel.: (416) 504-1657
www.poets.ca and www.youngpoets.ca
info@poets.ca

The League of Canadian Poets supports Canada's professional poetic community through activities that facilitate the teaching of Canadian poetry, develop audiences for poetry and encourage the publication, performance and recognition of Canadian poetry, nationally and internationally. It funds reading tours, publishes a guide to getting published and runs annual youth poetry contests.

Eligibility:
Depends on class of membership. Consult the website for more information.

Fees:
$175 for full members, $60 for associate members, and $20 for student members.

MAIN FILM

4067 St. Laurent Blvd., Suite 303, Montreal, QC H2V 3S4
Tel.: (514) 845-7442
www.mainfilm.qc.ca
info@mainfilm.qc.ca

Main Film is a service organization for independent filmmakers. It provides resources, equipment and space to independent movie and video producers and works to develop community interest in their work by organizing shows, seminars, conferences and research programs.

Eligibility:
Consult the website for information.

Fees:
$70 a year.

THE MONTREAL FILM AND TELEVISION COMMISSION

303 Notre Dame St. East, 6th Floor, Montreal, QC H2Y 3Y8
Tel.: (514) 872-2883
www.montrealfilm.com
film_tv@ville.montreal.qc.ca

The Montreal Film and Television Commission, part of the City of Montreal's Economic and Urban Development Department, coordinates all of the logistical aspects of film and television shoots on its territory and promotes Montreal to foreign producers as the best location for production and post-production.

PERIODICAL WRITERS ASSOCIATION OF CANADA (PWAC)

215 Spadina Ave., Suite 123, Toronto, ON M5T 2C7
Tel.: (416) 504-1645
www.pwac.ca and www.writers.ca
info@pwac.ca

PWAC is a network of freelance writers whose mandate is to develop and maintain professional standards in editor-writer relationships and encourage higher industry standards and fees for all types of freelance writing. Among its activities, it offers professional development workshops, hosts regular meetings and networking opportunities, and mediates grievances between writers and editors.

Fees:
They vary according to chapter. Consult the website for more information.

PLAYWRIGHTS GUILD OF CANADA (PGC)

54 Wolseley St., 2nd Floor, Toronto, ON M5T 1A5
Tel.: (416) 703-0201
www.playwrightsguild.ca
info@playwrightsguild.ca

The Playwrights Guild of Canada is a national association of professional and emerging playwrights. It provides a wide range of programs and services, including the promotion of its members' work through a catalogue and a Who's Who directory. It distributes professionally produced plays and offers agent services for professional and amateur productions.

Eligibility:

Full membership is reserved for professional playwrights who have had at least one play produced by a PACT-member theatre in the last ten years. Emerging playwrights whose work has received an advertised public staged reading are welcome to join as Associate Members.

Fees:

Full membership – $160.50
Associate membership – $69.55
Other services carry additional fees.

QUEBEC DRAMA FEDERATION (QDF)

460 Ste. Catherine St. West, Suite 807, Montreal, QC H3B 1A7
Tel.: (514) 875-8698
www.quebecdrama.org
qdf@cam.org

The Quebec Drama Federation sustains and supports the development of English-language theatre in Quebec through a combination of education, communication, professional training and networking initiatives. Members have access to professional development workshops, a Resource Centre, grant-writing consultations and referral services for performance/rehearsal spaces.

Eligibility:

Open to anybody with an interest in supporting English-language theatre in Quebec.

Fees:

Yes, though graduating CEGEP and university students receive a free one-year membership.

QUEBEC WRITERS' FEDERATION (QWF)

1200 Atwater Ave., Suite 3, Montreal, QC H3Z 1X4
Tel.: (514) 933-0878
www.qwf.org
info@qwf.org

The Quebec Writers' Federation promotes and encourages Quebec's English-language literary arts through a variety of activities that increase public awareness of the province's English-language literary arts community. It offers writers' workshops and a mentorship program, and maintains a database of books by English-language writers in Quebec. It also sponsors annual literary awards.

Eligibility:

Open to all, though some workshops are advanced.

Fees:

$20 a year for membership; $40 to $170 per workshop.

SAIDYE BRONFMAN CENTRE

5170 Cote St. Catherine Rd., Montreal, QC H3W 1M7
Tel.: (514) 339-2301
www.saidyebronfman.org
asirota@saidyebronfman.org

The Saidye Bronfman Centre provides activities in performance and
visual arts to people of all ages. Its services include a school of fine arts,
an English-language theatre, a Yiddish theatre troupe, and an art gallery.

Fees:
For courses and theatrical productions. Consult the website for more
information.

SOCIÉTÉ DES AUTEURS DE RADIO, TÉLÉVISION ET CINÉMA (SARTEC)

1229 Panet, Montreal, QC H2L 2Y6
Tel.: (514) 526-9196
www.sartec.qc.ca
information@sartec.qc.ca

SARTEC represents Canadian artists working in French in radio,
television, film and audiovisual arts. It supports the economic, social and
ethical interests of its members through a variety of services such as
script registration and collective insurance plans.

Eligibility:
Open to anybody who has signed a professional contract under
SARTEC's jurisdiction.

Fees:
Yes. Consult the website for more information.

SOCIÉTÉ DES AUTEURS ET COMPOSITEURS DRAMATIQUES (SACD)

4446 St. Laurent Blvd., Suite 202, Montreal, QC H2W 1Z5
Tel.: (514) 738-8877
www.sacd.ca

SACD is an authors' society that protects the rights of its members and
collects royalties for the use of their work. It offers its services in French
only.

SCULPTORS SOCIETY OF CANADA (SSC)

Studio: 204-60 Atlantic Ave., Toronto, ON M6K 1X9
Gallery: 64 Merton St., Toronto, ON M4S 1A1
Tel.: (416) 214-0389
www.cansculpt.org
gallery@cansculpt.org

The Sculptors Society of Canada promotes Canadian sculpture and sculptors nationally and internationally, and nurtures young talent, including graduating students and emerging sculptors. It offers a broad range of services, including lectures, seminars, workshops and studio tours, as well as curated exhibits of its members' work.

Eligibility:

Canadians working in sculpture who are no longer in school. Members are accepted by jury.

Fees:

Yes. Consult the website for more information.

TECHNOCOMPÉTENCES – COMITÉ SECTORIEL DE MAIN-D'OEUVRE EN TECHNOLOGIES DE L'INFORMATION ET DES COMMUNICATIONS

550 Sherbrooke St. West, Suite 100, Montreal, QC H3A 1B9
Tel.: (514) 840-1237
www.technocompetences.qc.ca
info@technocompetences.qc.ca

TECHNOCompétences supports and promotes the development of labour and employment in the information technology and communications industries, in conjunction with industry partners. It offers study reports on the labour force in these sectors, as well as occupation profiles and dictionaries of competencies.

WRITERS GUILD OF CANADA

366 Adelaide St. West, Suite 401, Toronto, ON M5V 1R9
Tel.: (416) 979-7907/1-800-567-9974
www.wgc.ca
info@wgc.ca

The Writers Guild of Canada represents more than 1,800 screenwriters working in television, film, radio and new media. The Guild negotiates on behalf of its members on matters concerning pay rates, contracts and working conditions for English-language productions in Canada, and is an advocate for screenwriters' rights. It administers a script registration service.

Eligibility:

At least one writing contract with a production company that is a signatory to our Voluntary Recognition Agreement.

Fees:

$350 initiation fee for new members; $150 annual dues, plus working fees.

YOUTH EMPLOYMENT SERVICES (YES)

630 René-Lévesque Blvd. West, Suite 185, Montreal, QC H3B 1S6
Tel.: (514) 878-9788
www.yesmontreal.ca
info@yesmontreal.ca

Youth Employment Services is a non-profit community organization that delivers English-language job-search and employment services to Quebecers. It offers a broad range of employment-related programs, including an Entrepreneurship Program for those looking to start or grow their own business and an Artists' Program, which is designed to help artists find work or create their own employment opportunities.

YES also offers grants of up to $5,000 for arts projects and loans of up to $15,000 for business-related projects. Consult the website for more information.

Eligibility:
The Entrepreneurship and Artists' Programs are open to all; job-search services, grants and loans are reserved for those aged 16 to 35.

Fees:
Minimal charges for workshops. Consult the website for more information.

GRANTING AGENCIES

BELL BROADCAST AND NEW MEDIA FUND/FONDS DE LA RADIODIFFUSION ET DES NOUVEAUX MÉDIAS DE BELL

4200 St. Laurent Blvd., Suite 503, Montreal, QC H2W 2R2
Tel.: (514) 845-4334
www.ipf.ca
fipinfo@ipf.ca

The Bell Broadcast and New Media Fund offers funding for television and feature-film projects.

Eligibility:
Consult the website for more information.

CANADA COUNCIL FOR THE ARTS

Address: 350 Albert St., P.O. Box 1074, Ottawa, ON K1P 5V8
Tel.: 1-800-263-5588 ext. 5060
www.canadacouncil.ca
info@canadacouncil.ca

The Canada Council for the Arts fosters and promotes the study and enjoyment of the arts. It offers more than 70 grants to professional Canadian artists, as well as a broad range of services.

Eligibility:
Applicants must be recognized as professional artists or professional arts organizations. Consult the website for more information.

CANADIAN HERITAGE

Guy-Favreau Complex, 200 René-Lévesque Blvd. West, West Tower, 6th Floor, Montreal, QC H2Z 1X4
Tel.: (514) 283-2332
www.pch.gc.ca

The Department of Canadian Heritage promotes Canadian content in entertainment and the arts, and fosters cultural participation among Canadians. It offers technical and financial support to non-profit organizations.

Eligibility:
Varies by program. Consult the website for more information.

THE CANADIAN INDEPENDENT FILM AND VIDEO FUND (CIFVF)

Suite 203, 666 Kirkwood Ave., Ottawa, ON K1Z 5X9
Tel.: (613) 729-1900
www.cifvf.ca
info@cifvf.ca

The CIFVF provides financial assistance to independent Canadian producers for the development and production of English and French films, videos and new media projects that promote lifelong learning.

Eligibility:
Please consult the website.

Fees:
$30 per application.

COGECO PROGRAM DEVELOPMENT FUND/FONDS COGECO DE DÉVELOPPEMENT D'ÉMISSION

4200 St. Laurent Blvd., Suite 503, Montreal, QC H2W 2R2
Tel.: (514) 845-4334
www.ipf.ca
fipinfo@ipf.ca

The Cogeco Program Development Fund offers funding for television and feature-film projects.

Eligibilty:
Consult the website for more information.

CONSEIL DES ARTS ET DES LETTRES DU QUÉBEC (CALQ)

Montreal address: 500 Place d'Armes, 15th Floor, Montreal, QC H2Y 2W2
Quebec City address: 79 René-Lévesque Blvd. East, 3rd Floor, Quebec, QC
G1R 5N5
Tel. (Montreal): (514) 864-3350 or 1 800 608-3350
Tel. (Quebec): (418) 643-1707 or 1 800 897-1707
www.calq.gouv.qc.ca
info@calq.gouv.qc.ca

CALQ is a government corporation dedicated to the development of the
arts and literature. It offers grants and assistance to professional artists
and non-profit cultural organizations working in the realms of the visual
arts, the arts and crafts, literature, performing arts, multidisciplinary arts,
media arts and architectural research.

Eligibility:
Open to professional artists and non-profit cultural organizations. Consult
the website for more information.

THE DANIEL LANGLOIS FOUNDATION FOR ART, SCIENCE AND TECHNOLOGY

3530 St. Laurent Blvd., Suite 402, Montreal, QC H2X 2V1
Tel.: (514) 987-7177
www.fondation-langlois.org
info@fondation-langlois.org

The Daniel Langlois Foundation for Art, Science and Technology fosters
the intersection of art and science in the field of technology by promoting
contemporary artistic practices that use digital technologies to express
aesthetic and critical forms of discourse. The Foundation has three
funding programs, one for individual artists and scientists, one for
organizations and one for researchers in residence at its Centre for
Research and Documentation, which can accommodate up to ten
researchers at a time.

Eligibility:
Consult the website for more information.

FONDATION DU MAIRE DE MONTRÉAL POUR LA JEUNESSE (FMMJ)

385 Sherbrooke St. East, Suite 800, Montreal, QC H2X 1E3
Tel.: (514) 872-8401
www.fondationdumaire.qc.ca
fondation@ville.montreal.qc.ca

The FMMJ offers low-income young Montrealers financial support to
start a business or launch a cultural project. Grant recipients may also

benefit from a wide range of technical and professional services as well as from the Foundation's outstanding network of contacts.

Eligibility:

Open to Canadian citizens aged 18 to 35 who have lived on the Island of Montreal for at least six months.

THE FOUNDATION TO ASSIST CANADIAN TALENT ON RECORDS (FACTOR)

355 King St. West, 5th Floor, Toronto, ON M5V 1J6
Tel.: (416) 351-1361
www.factor.ca
factor@factor.ca

FACTOR is dedicated to assisting the growth and development of Canada's independent recording industry. Grants and loans are offered to Canadian recording artists and songwriters to offset the costs of producing material, creating videos and touring. FACTOR also supports Canadian record labels, distributors, recording studios, video production companies, producers, engineers and directors.

Eligibility:

Varies by program. Consult the website for more information.

INDEPENDENT PRODUCTION FUND/FONDS INDÉPENDANT DE PRODUCTION

4200 St. Laurent Blvd., Suite 503, Montreal, QC H2W 2R2
Tel.: (514) 845-4334
www.ipf.ca
fipinfo@ipf.ca

The Independent Production Fund offers funding for television and feature-film projects.

Eligibilty:

Consult the website for more information.

SOCIÉTÉ DE DÉVELOPPEMENT DES ENTREPRISES CULTURELLES (SODEC)

215 rue St. Jacques St., Suite 800, Montreal, QC H2Y 1M6
Tel.: (514) 841-2200
www.sodec.gouv.qc.ca
info@sodec.gouv.qc.ca

SODEC provides assistance to Quebec's cultural enterprises.

Eligibility:

Open to all cultural enterprises in the province. Please consult the website for more information.

VIDÉOTRON FUND/FONDS VIDÉOTRON

1030 Cherrier, Suite 503, Montreal, QC H2L 1H9
Tel.: (514) 842-2497
www.fondsvideotron.ca
info@fondsvideotron.ca

The Vidéotron Fund promotes the production of Canadian television programs of an educational and educational/entertainment nature, as well as the production of interactive multimedia products that use information and communication technologies.

Eligibility:
Financing is restricted to television producers. Consult the website for more information.

FESTIVALS

ACREQ - ELEKTRA FESTIVAL

1908 Panet St., Suite 304, Montreal, QC H2L 3A2
Tel.: (514) 524-0208
www.elektrafestival.ca
info@elektrafestival.ca

The ACREQ - Elektra Festival is a presentation of electronic music and multimedia works.

Who can submit work:
Any artists involved in producing electronic music or multimedia.

Employment opportunities:
Development agents; marketing; press relations; production directors; technical directors; production assistants; sound and video directors; technicians; photographers; graphic designers.

Volunteer opportunities:
Audience surveys; reception.

FESTIVAL DE THÉÂTRE DES AMÉRIQUES (FTA)

C.P. 507, Succ. Desjardins, Montreal, QC H5B 1B6
Tel.: (514) 842-0704
www.fta.qc.ca

The Festival de Théâtre des Amériques is a festival of contemporary works that takes place in Montreal once every two years. It showcases innovative, creative artists who flaunt established codes and conventions.

Who can submit work:
Professional contemporary artists.

Volunteer opportunities:
Several functions in theatre venues, including hosts, ushers, program distributors, etc.

FESTIVAL INTERNATIONAL DE JAZZ DE MONTRÉAL

822 Sherbrooke St., East, Montreal, QC H2L 1K4
Tel.: (514) 523-3378
www.montrealjazzfest.com

Consult the website for more information about the festival's mandate, format, and employment and volunteer opportunities.

FESTIVAL INTERNATIONAL NUITS D'AFRIQUE

4374 St. Laurent Blvd., 1st Floor, Montreal, QC H2W 1Z5
Tel.: (514) 499-9239
info@festivalnuitsdafrique.com

The Festival International Nuits d'Afrique has carved out a unique position on the cultural landscape by showcasing the best of old and new world traditions in a spirit of magic and family-filled passion.

Who can submit work:
Any artist or group. Please send a CD, a press kit, promotional material, etc.

Volunteer opportunities:
A broad range of opportunities, including security, press relations, cleaning, etc.

IMAGE+NATION, MONTREAL INTERNATIONAL QUEER FILM FESTIVAL

4067 St. Laurent Blvd., Suite 404, Montreal, QC H2W 1Y7
Tel.: (514) 285 4467
www.image-nation.org
info@image-nation.org

Image+Nation is Montreal's International Lesbian and Gay Film and Video Festival and the largest and fastest growing festival of its kind in Canada. It brings together the best queer media works from around the globe for 11 days of exciting and moving queer images.

Who can submit work:
Anyone.

Employment opportunities:
Various possibilities in communications, film traffic, volunteer

coordination, theatre hosting, tickets sales coordination, etc.

Volunteer opportunities:
Tickets sales, program distribution, flyer distribution, poster distribution, theatre host, chauffeur, writing for program book and website, coordination of special events and galas.

INTERNATIONAL FESTIVAL OF FILMS ON ART

640 St. Paul St. West, Suite 406, Montreal, QC H3C 1L9
Tel.: (514) 874-1637
Fax: (514) 874-9929
www.artfifa.com
admin@artfifa.com

The International Festival of Films on Art features the screening of 250 English and French films related to a wide variety of art disciplines, including painting, dance, sculpture, architecture, design, theatre, photography, art history, cinema, literature and music.

Who can submit work:
Consult the website for more information.

Employment opportunities:
Positions are available through Emploi-Québec's employment programs. Candidates must meet Emploi-Québec's eligibility criteria.

Volunteer opportunities:
Cinema/theatre ushers, administrative support, etc.

LES JOURNÉES DE LA CULTURE

Secrétariat des Journées de la culture
4750 Henri-Julien Ave., Suite R-600, Montreal, QC H2T 2C8
Tel.: (514) 873-2641
www.journeesdelaculture.qc.ca
info@journeesdelaculture.qc.ca

Les Journées de la Culture is a yearly celebration of Quebec culture that strives to promote public awareness in art through three days of free activities.

Who can submit work:
Artists, artisans and other people involved in the cultural milieu who are willing to complete projects on a volunteer basis.

MAIN MADNESS

Société de développement du boulevard Saint-Laurent
4398 St. Laurent Blvd., Suite 309, Montreal, QC H2W 1Z5
Tel.: (514) 286-0334
www.boulevardsaintlaurent.com

Every year, St. Laurent Boulevard marks the coming of summer by transforming itself into a huge open-air market. Three hundred merchants offer visitors thousands of irresistible bargains on hundreds of items and services.

Who can submit work:
Only artists who have been issued a permit by the City of Montreal may showcase their work. Those selected must purchase a licence in order to sell their work.

Volunteer opportunities:
Information and reception, logistic assistant, support activities.

MUTEK – MUSIC, SOUND AND NEW TECHNOLOGIES

Ex-Centris
3530 St. Laurent Blvd., Suite 406, Montreal, QC H2X 2V1
Tel.: (514) 847-3536
www.mutek.ca
info@mutek.ca

MUTEK is an organization dedicated to showcasing emerging forms of electronic music and sound creation. The annual five-day MUTEK festival introduces the public to this genre of music production and acts as a springboard for a new generation of the field's most innovative and visionary artists.

Who can submit work:
Cutting edge musicians and audiovisual artists with a strong artistic background.

Volunteer opportunities:
Logistics; marketing and communications; office work; surveys; box office, etc.

LE MOIS DE LA PHOTO À MONTRÉAL

460 St. Catherine St. West, Suite 320, Montreal, QC H3B 1A7
Tel.: (514) 390-0383
www.moisdelaphoto.com

The Mois de la Photo à Montréal is a major, biennial international event focused on issues relating to contemporary photography. Bringing together artists, curators and other specialists, it creates a unique and exciting opportunity for studying the transformations of the image in our contemporary culture.

Who can submit work:
Anyone. Consult the website for more information.

MONTREAL JEWISH FILM FESTIVAL/FESTIVAL DU FILM JUIF DE MONTRÉAL

1564 St. Denis, Montreal, QC H2X 3K2
Tel.: (514) 987-9795
www.mjff.qc.ca

The Montreal Jewish Film Festival showcases exceptional films that celebrate the diversity of the Jewish experience around the world.

Who can submit work:
Anyone, but films and videos must have Jewish content. Works can be in any language, but must have French and/or English subtitles.

Employment opportunities:
Please enquire in February or consult the website for more information.

Volunteer opportunities:
Please enquire in February or consult the website for more information.

MONTREAL NEW CINEMA FESTIVAL/FESTIVAL DU NOUVEAU CINÉMA DE MONTRÉAL

3530 St. Laurent Blvd., Suite 304, Montreal, QC H2X 2V1
Tel.: (514) 847-9272
www.fcmm.com
info@fcmm.com

The Montreal New Cinema Festival presents feature films and videos, documentaries, shorts and new media works. The festival organizes a series of special events aimed at promoting selected works, including press screenings, promotional evenings and a professional forum.

Who can submit work:
All formats and genres are accepted. Only works produced after January 1 of the previous year are eligible. Works must not have been shown previously in Quebec. All selected entries must be in their original language and subtitled in French (preferably) or English.

POP MONTREAL

15 Mont-Royal St. West, Suite 110, Montreal, QC H2T 2R9
Tel.: (514) 842-1919
www.popmontreal.com
info@popmontreal.com

POP Montreal is a four-day international pop music festival that pays special attention to iconic pop performances, taste-making labels, and groundbreaking artists. Taking place mainly in the Plateau, the event features shows pairing international stars with the best acts from Quebec and Canada, numerous industry events, and late-night loft parties that go well into the wee hours of the morning.

Who can submit work:
Anyone can submit an application to POP Montreal, but there are only a limited number of spots. Each application is listened to carefully, whether the band or artist has released several albums or none.

Volunteer opportunities:
Ample opportunities, including security, ushering, registration coordination and clerical duties.

LES RENCONTRES INTERNATIONALES DU DOCUMENTAIRE DE MONTRÉAL (RIDM)

5455 de Gaspé Ave., Suite 1104, Montréal, QC H2T 3B3
Tel.: (514) 499-3676
www.ridm.qc.ca

The RIDM is an annual event dedicated to promoting the creation, production and distribution of point-of-view documentary films. The RIDM offers a space for reflection and encourages dialogue and debates between the audience, the artists and the many professionals concerned by stories of reality.

Who can submit work:
Consult the website for regulations.

Volunteer opportunities:
Openings for anybody who is interested in learning more about the organization of a film festival.

SALON DU LIVRE DE MONTRÉAL

480 St. Laurent Blvd., Suite 403, Montreal, QC H2Y 3Y7
Tel.: (514) 845-2365
www.salondulivredemontreal.com

The Salon du Livre de Montréal is an annual public event that promotes reading while fostering interaction between the general public and regional, national and international publishers. The event fosters the development of relationships among publishers, booksellers and libraries and serves as a direct promotional tool for vendors to sell their books on location.

Who can submit work:
Publishers and distributors.

Employment opportunities:
About 40 people are hired for the five-day event.

SENSATION MODE

3981 St. Laurent Blvd., Suite 506, Montreal, QC H2W 1Y5
Tel.: (514) 876-1499
www.sensationmode.com
jramos@sensationmode.com

Sensation Mode strives to promote Quebec designers and artists through its celebration of fashion and design.

ST-AMBROISE MONTRÉAL FRINGE® FESTIVAL

c/o Théâtre MainLine Theatre
C.P. 42013, succ. Jeanne-Mance, Montréal, QC H2W 2T3
Tel.: (514) 849-3378
www.fringemontreal.ca
fringe@montrealfringe.ca

The annual Montreal Fringe Festival is an 11-day celebration of creative energy. Over 60 artistic companies from North America and the UK join together for the entertainment of an equally international audience.

Who can submit an application:
Theatre companies and performers, on a first-come, first-served basis. Consult the website for more information.

WORLD FILM FESTIVAL OF MONTREAL/FESTIVAL DES FILMS DU MONDE DE MONTRÉAL

1432 de Bleury Street, Montreal, QC H3A 2J1
Tel.: (514) 848-3883
www.ffm-montreal.org
info@ffm-montreal.org

Every year, films from more than 70 countries, including well-known and first-time filmmakers alike, are selected to appear at the World Film Festival of Montreal. Many films have been discovered in Montreal.

Who can submit work:
Consult the website for more information.

BIOGRAPHIES

SUSAN MOLNAR, Arts Program Director and Career Counsellor at YES from 1998 to 2004, created a cutting edge employment program for self-employed artists. This book was conceived as a natural extension to over 50 workshops and conferences that focused on business skills for artists and united emerging and professional artistic communities in Montreal. She received her Bachelor's in Philosophy (textile design cluster) from Concordia and her Master's in Education (Counselling Psychology) from McGill.

DANIELLE PITL graduated from Concordia University with a Joint Specialization in English and History and a minor in Liberal Arts in 2003. During the last year of her BA, as an intern at Shoreline Press, she edited *Spiral Road*, the memoirs of Mrs. Laurel Buck. She worked at McGill-Queen's University Press for a year following graduation. She has contributed to Business Skills for Creative Souls as an interviewer, a researcher and an editor.

CARALEE SALOMON's Grade 4 teacher once wrote of her student that "writing isn't her field." Well! Caralee went on to obtain a degree in Journalism and Communication Studies from Concordia University and has been publishing her work ever since. Still wary of Mme. Forget's fourth grade assessment, mind you, she now studies law at Université de Montréal.

MARK SHAINBLUM is an award-winning author and editor perhaps best-known in Montreal as the writer and co-creator of the popular comic strip *Angloman*. Over the last several years he has served as Head Writer of Montreal-based Airborne Entertainment and Editor-in-Chief of English Publications at Les éditions Ma Carrière (now known as Jobboom). He has published extensively in the fields of journalism, science fiction and comic books and is past-president of SF Canada, Canada's national association of science fiction authors.

RACHEL STEPHAN holds a Master's Degree in Graphic Arts and Advertising from l'*Université du St-Esprit* in Lebanon. Rachel has a unique and varied career path and has over 10 years of experience working in advertising agencies, publishing houses and, since 2001, running her own company, les sens créatifs inc.

Rachel is a member of l'*Association des professionels en expositions du Québec (APEQ)* and serves as a member of the planning committee of APEQ's annual conference.

Rachel is also an active member of TELUS-Québec's annual Gala to benefit the Share the Warmth Foundation, which she serves as a member of the board of directors.

Additionally, Rachel serves as President of the Marketing Group, which organizes networking and business development events in Montreal.